Toward a Learning Society

ALTERNATIVE CHANNELS TO LIFE, WORK, AND SERVICE

A Report and Recommendations by
The Carnegie Commission on Higher Education
OCTOBER 1973

MCGRAW-HILL BOOK COMPANY
New York   St. Louis   San Francisco   Düsseldorf
London   Sydney   Toronto   Mexico   Panama
Johannesburg   Kuala Lumpur   Montreal
New Delhi   São Paulo   Singapore

*This report is issued by the Carnegie Commission
on Higher Education, with headquarters at
2150 Shattuck Avenue, Berkeley, California 94704.
The views and conclusions expressed in this report
are solely those of the members of the Carnegie Commission
on Higher Education and do not necessarily reflect the
views or opinions of the Carnegie Corporation of New York,
The Carnegie Foundation for the Advancement of Teaching,
or their trustees, officers, directors, or employees.*

Library of Congress Cataloging in Publication Data

Carnegie Commission on Higher Education.
    Toward a learning society.

    Bibliography: p.
    1. Education, Higher—1965–   2. Adult
education. I. Title.
LB2322.C37   1973   378   73-15991
ISBN 0-07-010101-9

Additional copies of this report may be ordered from
McGraw-Hill Book Company, Hightstown, New Jersey 08520.
The price is $2.95 a copy.

Contents

The vision of the learning society . . . can be realized. A world community learning to be civilized, learning to be human, is at last a possibility. Education may come into its own.

ROBERT M. HUTCHINS
The Learning Society

Work has a greater effect than any other technique of living in the direction of binding the individual more closely to society.

SIGMUND FREUD
Civilization and Its
Discontents

Sometimes give your services for nothing . . .

HIPPOCRATES
Precepts

No pleasure endures unseasoned by variety.

PUBLIUS SYRUS
Maxim 406

Foreword

Education is too often perceived as an activity that occurs only at certain times in people's lives, in certain institutional settings, at certain times of the day, and in a certain few accepted formats. At the postsecondary level, education is most immediately thought of in terms of colleges and universities—the institutions of higher education that have been central to the concerns of this Commission for more than five years.

In this report, we expand our frame of reference, because our colleges and universities operate in an educational environment that includes not only them but also thousands of other educational or quasi-educational institutions and programs. There is an enormous range of purposes, of levels, and rigor of instruction in these other institutions and programs, and most of them are quite different from colleges and universities. But there is a considerable overlap of educational activity between the colleges and other sectors of education, and, for certain subjects and certain students, these channels to life and learning outside the colleges are often — or should often be—the preferred sources of education beyond high school. Moreover, in its drive to provide access for its citizens to any level of education commensurate with their ability and potential benefit, American society must make flexible yet responsible use of the fullest range of its available institutional resources for education. The diversity of our postsecondary educational system and our capacity as a nation to realize the ideal of a society in which learning throughout the lives of all persons is a highly valued and widely pursued endeavor depend heavily on such efforts.

We see in postsecondary education today many signs that our institutions of learning are becoming increasingly adaptable to the service of a learning society. Access to education is increasing, not only for persons who come from economically disadvantaged families, but also for persons whose early education was inadequate, for persons who are beyond the traditional age of school attendance, and for persons who encounter the need for recurrent learning throughout their lives. Some institutions, also, are introducing greater flexibility into the patterns they devise for teaching and learning.

In this report, we discuss the problems and opportunities these new developments have generated. We also give attention to institutions other than colleges and universities that provide postsecondary education. By so doing, we hope to:

- Identify a variety of channels that provide alternatives or supplements to the college experience

- Consider ways in which the alternative channels might be more fully meshed into the total postsecondary educational system while still preserving diversity

- Examine the postsecondary educational activities of the high school graduates who do not go on to college

- Examine learning activities in their relationship to preparation for work

- Consider special problems such as accreditation, student counseling, and public subsidization, as they are related to these alternative channels

Progress in these areas would help advance us toward realization of a society somewhat similar to that envisaged by Robert M. Hutchins in his essay on *The Learning Society*. He described that society as one which "in addition to offering part-time adult education to every man and woman at every stage in grown-up life, has succeeded in transforming its values in such a way that learning, fulfillment, becoming human, has become its aim and all its institutions were directed to this end" (Hutchins, 1968, p. 134). We define "learning," however, more broadly than does Hutchins to include technical training and other quasi-academic and even nonacademic programs. No doubt, in some sense, everything adults, as well as children, do contributes in some way to their development although there are immense variations in curiosity, openness, and ability to profit intellectually and morally from work, family life, voluntary associational activities, and so on. Moreover, Hutchins' implication that work will not play a major role in life seems a misjudgment to us. Work will continue to be the central focus of life for most men and perhaps a majority of women if one thinks of work outside the home, and for virtually all women if one thinks of work inside the home as well. Nevertheless, many current trends appear to be in the direction of a society considerably more devoted than ours is now to the continuation of learning in a formal sense.

Much remains to be done, however, by institutions of learning and by those who formulate educational policies for our cities, states, and nation if ample learning opportunity is to be fully available to all who can take advantage of it, if all the appropriate educational channels to life and work are to be effectively utilized, if our institutions of learning are to become sufficiently flexible to accommodate new types of learners, and if learning throughout life is to become a more significant characteristic of American society.

In previous reports of the Commission, we have stated some of our major conclusions as recommendations. In this report we depart from that practice. Some of the desired outcomes of the trends we discuss here depend not only upon specific actions but also upon the influence of other general developments taking place in postsecondary education, and the direction of many of these developments is not yet certain. It seems appropriate, therefore, to speak less of recommendations than of objectives, keeping opportunities open for flexible responses to events. We identify two types of objectives — (1) those that are *specific* in that they relate to particular conditions or channels of postsecondary education, and (2) those that are *general* in that they relate to broader questions and concerns.

The subjects discussed in this report are not entirely new to us:

- In our report *Less Time, More Options: Education Beyond the High School,* one of the major themes was that "higher education and the degrees it affords should be available to persons throughout their lifetimes and not just immediately after high school."

- In a more recent report, *The Campus and the City: Maximizing Assets and Reducing Liabilities,* we called for more dynamic relationships between institutions of higher learning and the metropolitan areas in which they are located. In that report, attention was given to educational services that should be extended to adults as well as to the youth of our cities.

- In *From Isolation to Mainstream: Problems of the Colleges Founded for Negroes,* we urged that more of the black colleges than do now should develop adult education programs that meet the particular needs of older residents in the communities they serve.

- In *Higher Education and the Nation's Health,* we recommended that "Continuing education of health manpower should be a major concern of the university health science centers and area health education centers. . . ."

- We recommended that adult education have an important role in the programs of the nation's two-year community colleges in *The Open-Door Colleges: Policies for Community Colleges.*

- More flexible educational programs were also discussed in *Reform on Campus: Changing Students, Changing Academic Programs,* and in *The Fourth Revolution: Instructional Technology in Higher Education.*

We have not earlier, however, looked at postsecondary education in its entirety. This reflects the attention to higher education in our founding charter as a commission on higher education. It also reflects the only recent realization by us, and by many others, of the actual and potential importance of elements of postsecondary education in addition to colleges and universities. There are many advantages to taking the more total view of education beyond the high school, as we shall indicate in what follows.

This report takes into consideration the findings and recommendations of other persons and organizations that have devoted time and attention to the goal of making postsecondary education in the United States at once more available to our population and more flexible for those who participate in its offerings. We wish to acknowledge, particularly, the contributions of the Commission on Non-Traditional Study, which completed its deliberations earlier this year. The report of this commission and its related research documents are certain to have great impact on decisions in this field for many years to come. We have also found particularly useful the American Council on Education's *Special Report on Higher Education and the Adult Student.*

Many people have contributed directly to the development of this report by providing information and reviewing and commenting upon its various drafts. We wish to express our appreciation to them for their valuable assistance.

We also wish to express appreciation to members of our staff and particularly to Verne A. Stadtman, John R. Shea, Allan M. Cartter, and Virginia B. Smith for their assistance in preparing this report.

Eric Ashby
The Master
Clare College
Cambridge, England

Ralph M. Besse
Partner
Squire, Sanders & Dempsey,
Counsellors at Law

1. Major Themes

1   We should be more concerned than we have been as a nation with the totality of endeavors leading to the advanced education of Americans; more with all the people to be served; more with the many channels to postsecondary education and training. Academic degree-credit instruction for full-time students is an absolutely essential part of the whole, but it is not by any means the sum total of the formal education of Americans beyond the high school (see Chart 1). Service to part-time degree-credit and to non-degree-credit students within higher education, and to students in the many institutions outside higher education, deserves comparatively more consideration. This consideration should be given without in any way diverting attention and support away from the more traditional forms of higher education. This report is primarily concerned with *(a)* the place of "nontraditional" students within higher education and *(b)* the enhanced role of "further education."

2   We favor universal access to higher education but oppose pressures that operate in the direction of universal attendance. College is not for everybody:

- At least 5 percent of all college students were "reluctant" attenders, and perhaps as high as 12 percent were to some degree, during a recent period when, among other factors, the military draft was still in effect. This is good neither for the reluctant attenders nor for the colleges they attend. Nearly another 20 percent of the students were only "marginally committed" in their attendance.

- Under conditions approaching universal attendance, the labor market would be quite saturated with college graduates. It is now failing to absorb, in positions that utilize their training, some of the graduates that result from a policy of universal access.

CHART 1 *The system of postsecondary education in the United States, 1970, on a full-time-equivalent basis*

Higher education

  *Full-time degree-
  credit students*　　　　　　　　　51.2 percent

  *Part-time and non-
  degree-credit students*　　　　11.2 percent

Further education

  Employers and unions　　　15.6 percent

  Private specialty schools　　8.2 percent

  Armed forces　　　6.9 percent

  *Elementary and secondary
  schools and other public
  postsecondary programs*　　3.6 percent

  All other　　3.3 percent

SOURCE: Table 5.

- A program of universal attendance would be costly and may be very wasteful of resources.[1]

- More students would be likely to drop out, under conditions approaching universal attendance, and the dropout rate in four-year institutions already runs in the range of 40 to 50 percent. Many such dropouts represent, to one degree or another, a failure of individual expectations or a disappointment with the contact with higher education.

- Too few young people now have contact with work, have any direct experience with production. They often do not, any longer, even see their parents at gainful work. Yet work is a tie to reality. If everybody were to go to college, then even those who now go would be likely to have less contact with work experience since work would be less of an accepted way for members of the age group to spend their time. Work would be even less a natural component of youth.

A point-of-no-return could be reached (it has already been reached in some situations) when higher education becomes "socially" compulsory, although this is not highly likely to happen nationwide; when nearly all young persons, for the sake of self-

[1] "Low achievers" in particular "are unlikely to benefit financially." (See W. Lee Hansen and Burton A. Weisbrod, "Schooling and Earnings of Low Achievers," *American Economic Review,* June 1970.)

defense in the labor market and for the sake of peer group conformity, if for no other reason, go to college. College attendance would then represent for many an attempt at protection against unemployment in competition with other college attenders, if employers were to continue to use it as a screening device, even though it added nothing to the totality of skills actually used. College attendance for some would be only a passport to the "queue line" for noncollege jobs. No additional economic outputs to society would result, only inputs of time and resources—the economic output curve related to more higher education would flatten out. The closer society gets to universal attendance in college, the more likely it is to move the whole way—an eventuality fraught with danger under current conditions of a moderately close connection between college attendance and labor market prospects.

3 Some form of education beyond high school levels, may well come to be for nearly everybody. We favor a whole series of improved channels, for access to such educational opportunities by all persons beyond high school age:

- Many people want such opportunities to improve their occupational prospects and the quality of their lives.

- A more complex society requires higher and ever newer skills, and more understanding of civic responsibilities.

- Society has the wealth to provide such opportunities, and individuals have the leisure and the prior education to take advantage of them.

4 We define:

Postsecondary education as all education beyond high school.

Higher education as oriented toward academic degrees or broad occupational certificates. It takes place on college or university campuses or through campus-substitute institutions, such as the "open university" with its "external degrees."

Further education as oriented toward more specific occupational or life skills, rather than academic degrees. It takes place in many noncampus environments—industry, trade unions, the military, proprietary vocational schools, among others.

5 We believe that the current system of postsecondary education in the United States has these deficiencies:

- It puts too much pressure on too many young people to attend college whether they want to or not. It offers them too few alternative options. It is thus biased too much toward academic subjects alone.

- It puts too much emphasis on continuation of education right after high school and then never again, rather than on learning throughout life. It thus discourages deferred attendance and the participation of older persons.

- It subsidizes college attendance far more favorably than it does other forms of education. It is thus biased by class, since the middle class is more likely to go to college; by type of job, since college tends to lead to the professions and to the higher-level white-collar occupations; and by age, since younger persons are the more frequent regular college enrollees.

6 The system can be improved by:

- Opening up more options for young people, including participation in:

  College

  Private specialty schools

  Educational programs in industry, trade unions, the military

  National service programs

- Creating more opportunities for returnees to higher education and for all adults to participate in postsecondary education

- Providing appropriate financial support for individuals and for institutions engaged in a wider variety of educational activities — and thus a greater sense of equity among individuals and competitive institutions

7 This reorganized system with more diverse opportunities would have these advantages in addition to providing more options for more people:

- It would make it more possible to mix education, work, and service in a more rounded experience for young people.

- It would help to mix the age groups in educational institutions to the benefit of individuals and to the end of their greater mutual understanding. It would reduce the age stratification that now takes place. In particular, it would help older persons to meet youth and to see the classroom and the campus environment through direct experience.

- It would reduce the burden on colleges to accept reluctant attenders since there would be more other opportunities for them, and to engage in programs of doubtful academic validity since other institutions would be better able to offer them.

8 Specifically we propose:

- More options for young persons to choose among education, work, and service, and to alternate among them. This means chances to "stop-out" between high school and college, and while in college. This also suggests the desirability of shorter "modules" of learning —we have proposed that a degree be available after each two-year module in colleges and universities.

- Extension of national service programs; and of educational opportunities in industry, trade unions, and the military.

- More opportunities in colleges for part-time and for adult students. This means reducing current barriers in admission policies, in fee structures, in course load requirements, in scheduling of classes, in faculty attitudes against the "nontraditional" student. It also means more "short-cycle" programs.

- The spread of community colleges within commuting distance of 95 percent of all Americans.

- The creation of "Learning Pavilions" in densely populated neighborhoods where people can drop in to study and to discuss their studies.

- Development of new educational opportunities such as in specialized "open universities," and in other external degree programs. The new electronic technology makes such opportunities much more possible. Important aspects of advanced education can now become both space-free and time-free—available anywhere, any time. These external degree programs are, however, in an experimental period of development, and neither their attractiveness nor their quality has as yet been fully demonstrated.

- Long-term consideration of an "educational endowment" or provision of "two years in the bank," as we once called it, that will guarantee financial access to postsecondary educational opportunities to all persons at whatever stage in life they want access to them. Along with this would go consideration of educational leaves from industry and government.

- More emphasis on a cumulative record of achievement and less on the academic degree by itself. This cumulative record would show achievements other than class grades and degrees alone, including credit by examination, extracurricular activities, service experience, and so forth. This would provide a broader view of the individual's accomplishments. It would also put less emphasis upon completion of a set number of hours of credit at a single institution. It would thus reduce the stigma of being a dropout. The penalty for dropping out is now often substantial. The cumulative record would show what had actually been accomplished and place less emphasis, for example, on whether it added up to 120 credit hours (and thus a degree) or only 100 credit hours (and thus no degree). In any event, the transcript of courses taken and grades earned is a more informative document than the certificate or degree by itself. We are suggesting an expanded version of the transcript with enhanced attention to other methods of accomplishment in addition to the receipt of a degree or even in lieu of a degree.

9 There are major problems with these proposals, just as there are with the current arrangements:

Will older adults mix well with youth? They may be handicapped by less inclination toward theory and by less retentive memories, but they will often bring greater motivation and more judgment based upon experience. The GI's after World War II were excellent students and raised the level of academic effort of all students. They were, however, only a few years older than other students.

Will general education suffer? It may, because some students now given access to it will choose channels that do not have a general education component. But many choose such channels now, or are even forced into them—such as the involuntarily chosen channel of unemployment. One answer is that a greater effort at general education should be made in the high school in any event. Short-cycle education, nevertheless, is more adapted to specific skill and knowledge training than it is to general education.

May continuity of academic effort be lost because of stopouts? It can be in areas where such continuity is important, as in the sciences and mathematics, and students in such areas may be well advised to pursue their work straight through. This would, of course, continue to be an available option as it now is.

Can a good national service system be developed? We recognize the problems of developing a large bureaucracy to administer it and of selection of projects that will draw forth the effort of young persons. We suggest that the federal government be involved in funding and in setting certain standards, but that actual programs be conducted by state and local agencies, or by selected individual federal agencies like the Forest Service, and by nonprofit organizations, rather than by one national agency. In any event, expansion should go slowly and be based on accumulating experience.

Will there be demands for academic credit for experiential learning? There are already. We oppose such credit unless there is a strong academic component, as in reading and in writing reports, or in taking academically oriented tests.

Will academic standards deteriorate? They need not. In fact, creating alternative channels for reluctant attenders may have the impact of raising standards for academic degrees; encouraging the attendance of persons after they have more maturity and greater motivation, as in the case of GI's, may have the same effect.

How may the enlarged system be subject to accreditation? We suggest two systems of accreditation or validation: one by government (validation) to protect consumers against fraud and taxpayers against wrongful use of public money; and the other by academic agencies (academic accreditation), as now, to assist in the evaluation of transcripts in transfers from one institution to another and at the point of entry into graduate school. Two systems of formal certification are required to serve two different sets of purposes, to reflect two different sets of standards, and to respond to two different sets of authorities. Public authorities would validate for public purposes, and the academic guild would accredit for guild purposes. The most important system of accreditation, in any event, will continue to be the informal one by students, professors, and employers—by the market, aided by counseling and advisory services.

Will employers be willing to accept cumulative records as well as degrees earned? That remains to be seen. The degree does speak to diligence and persistence in achieving a goal in a way that the cumulative record does not so quickly and so specifically. The cumulative record, however, can offer broader information and is fairer to more people, some of whom otherwise may be eliminated on quite artificial grounds. The evaluation of an extended transcript, however, is more time-consuming and involves more judgment than notation of a degree earned.

Will the academic world accept the introduction of the cumulative record? This is much more doubtful. The degree is well-rooted in history. It stands for a totality which may be greater than the sum of individual parts, if the total has been carefully planned by academic authorities; in some instances, as a medical degree, completion of the total program is absolutely essential. Fragmentation of learning is a very real concern, but its sources lie very deep and go back a long way in academic history—thus, while the use of a cumulative record might add to, it would not cause fragmentation. The degree also is an instrument of discipline.

Will the system as envisaged cost a great deal more than the present system? It will bring in more people and thus add to costs—we estimate $600 million annually by 1980 within higher education. We also estimate the annual cost of a system of Learning Pavilions as between $50 and $60 million by 1980. A well-developed program of national service will also be expensive. We do not have cost estimates on other aspects of the system as proposed; some of them, of course, involve no monetary expenditures at all.

Will there be greater administrative complexity? The answer is in the affirmative. Handling deferred admissions, stop-outs, and part-time students, as examples, does add to administrative burdens, as does the evaluation of more complicated transcripts.

How may the system be coordinated? It will be difficult. We suggest some overall mechanism at the state level to coordinate and plan for all postsecondary education with subsidiary mechanisms for *(a)* higher education and *(b)* for further education. The two should not be handled entirely together since quite different types of institutions, financing arrangements, and student-body and faculty constituencies are involved. Higher education, in turn, may best be coordinated, at least in part, segment by segment rather than all segments together. Coordination, in any event, should involve planning and cooperative arrangements, and not detailed administration.

10 Much of the framework for an extended postsecondary system, as we see it, already exists, as do many of the facilities. About one-half of the total system, on a full-time equivalent basis and not a head-count basis, as it is now composed, consists of "traditional" students on campus and around another 10 percent of "nontraditional" students, for a total of roughly 60 percent of the FTE's through colleges and universities. Other substantial components are provided by private specialty schools (about 10 percent), by industry and unions (about 15 percent), and by the armed services (over 5 percent), with the other approximately 10 percent more widely scattered (see Chart 1 above).

The course for the future holds at least three major possibilities:

Continuation of current patterns

Greater concentration on higher education if we move toward universal attendance in college

Some comparative elevation of the attractiveness of alternative channels, while improving higher education

We generally favor the third course. We should not overload higher education and we should protect its quality. Nor need everyone go through the same set of institutions. If we should end up with only one preferred channel into life and work, and if that channel should be internally homogenized, as some current trends portend, then we are in for real trouble in many aspects of society. There once were many streams into life and work—through the family as the farmer's son became a farmer, through apprenticeship in order to enter a craft, through inservice training as in a lawyer's office, and through many other social mechanisms. We consider it a wiser course to continue with many streams to accommodate the different interests and abilities of individuals and the varying requirements of society.

11 Much of the financial structure is also now in place:

Low- or no-tuition community colleges

Basic opportunity grants, work-study programs, and loans for students (although each program needs improvement)

Financial credit for education following military service

Financial assistance for dependents of social security recipients

We suggest *(a)* that existing support programs be spread out to cover more types of students and more types of programs and *(b)* that educational benefits be given also for participation in national service programs.

We also suggest development of programs in industry for educational leaves, as in France, and consideration of an "educational security" program, on a contributory basis, to extend the directions set by the development of unemployment compensation, old age security, and medical security programs. Such an "educational security" program could be particularly useful for employed adults, in connection with educational leaves, to give them a better chance to gain additional educational opportunities. Any unused portions could be added to social security benefits.

We recognize that most postsecondary education will still tend to take place at the younger ages since *(a)* subsistence costs are lower, *(b)* the cost of forgone earnings is smaller, *(c)* the "payoff" period for the education is longer, and *(d)* there is less disruption of family life.

12 Working out the division of labor in this expanded system is of great importance. We see the following elements with their prospective rates of expansion:

Traditional students — usually accepted as meaning full-time, degree-credit students, mostly young and attending in the daytime and on campus. Moderate expansion in the 1970s and no expansion in the 1980s.

Nontraditional students — defined as young and older part-time degree-credit and non-degree-credit students attending often in the evening and in off-campus as well as on-campus locations. Substantial expansion from the current base in the 1970s but particularly in the 1980s.

Academic programs — defined as programs that normally lead to a degree that requires courses outside the subject field of specialization. Moderate expansion in the 1970s but no expansion in the 1980s even with the addition of more nontraditional students.

Quasi-academic or *nonacademic programs* — defined as programs of several types: *(a)* specific occupational skill training, *(b)* specific nonoccupational skill and knowledge training as in leisure-time activities, *(c)* "sensate" or emotional training as in the Esalen Institute, and *(d)* "experiential" programs that give credit for nonacademic work or service or travel or other experience. Substantial expansion in the future for each of these four areas.

There is a very real difference in kind, and not just in degree, between academic programs on the one hand, and specific technical training "arts and crafts" type work programs that appeal to the "sensate" impulses and "life experiences" on the other—much as the latter four also each differ from each other.

We suggest that higher education concentrate on academic and broad occupational programs, adding more nontraditional students. College-substitute institutions, like "open universities," should particularly concentrate on nontraditional students. Colleges, if they are to serve nontraditional students well and to compete for them successfully, will need to give them first-class treatment rather than the second-class attention now too often accorded them.

We suggest that further education can concentrate best on quasi-academic and nonacademic programs, and thus, also, mostly on nontraditional students.

The community colleges often live in both the worlds of higher and of further education and constitute a connecting element between them. They are an expanding sector of higher education partly because they serve nontraditional students more and also provide more quasi-academic programs than other segments do.

We believe that public subsidy is better concentrated on academic programs and on specialized technical programs of type *(a)* than on largely nonacademic programs *(b), (c)* and *(d),* which should be supported with public funds only under specially chosen circumstances.

The prospects for growth for higher education are greater for nontraditional than for traditional students; and for further education are more substantial than for higher education. Higher education will expand in total enrollments in the 1970s, and then decrease in the 1980s; and it will be an increasingly smaller proportion of postsecondary education as further education expands more rapidly.

13 Courses of development for the future, we believe, lie substantially in the directions set forth in this report:

- New clienteles are developing for postsecondary education— persons who missed advanced education earlier in life and would like access to it now; women who have raised their children and now want to enter a career; persons who want to change their occupations or to update their skills and knowledge—to avoid becoming obsolete; persons who want to understand their personal situations better as, for example, in adjusting to a serious operation; persons who are ill or handicapped or isolated and want to add education to the interests of their lives; all those who want to "stop-in" into advanced education. We believe there is now a major degree of underconsumption of education by members of such groups.

- Postsecondary education can be helpful as a mechanism for handling several of the discontinuities of life in a dignified and useful way—reentry into the labor force, changed positions in the labor force, retirement, a sharp break in life status. Education can play a role in the development of new patterns of life, new rhythms of life mixing education, work, and leisure. More women than men are likely to find these opportunities beneficial. More of them missed their earlier chances. More of them have their lives interrupted by childbearing and child-rearing.

- The period of "youth" is changing. It is being prolonged by affluence and by changes in the expectations of and opportunities in the labor market; it starts earlier and ends later. It is being changed by demands of young persons for better chances to test out and to evaluate alternative options among careers and lifestyles. It is being experienced by more young people in the sense that more of them now have a "free choice" period between high school and first job or marriage. More of young people, also, are "sliders" descending the socioeconomic staircase, and it takes time to make the descent and it involves special problems. The transition from childhood to adulthood is now longer for most young persons and more difficult for many of them than it was in the simpler society of the past. Postsecondary education for some is a straight track into an occupation, for others a chance to look around intellectually and occupationally, for others a graceful way to slide away from parental expectations, for some an alternative to unemployment; it serves several purposes for a diverse group of people. We need better and more varied methods to provide opportunities for youth to learn, to work, to serve. The family is less in charge of this transitional period, and education more. Any culture must be concerned with how best to initiate youth into work and life.

- The labor market is changing. It requires more skills, and new skills. It is more dynamic. It is harder for students to aim at, and adults to stay in, one occupation. Sweden has pioneered with an "active labor market policy"; and it now costs 2 to 3 percent of the GNP. This policy provides, among other things, for reeducation during periods of unemployment. The United States is moving in the same direction. Postsecondary education can be utilized as a counter-cyclical device, taking up the slack in the labor market in recession and providing a reservoir of persons for expansion.

- The new technology potentially turns every home into a classroom.

- Supply creates its own demand. The more education the parents have, the more they want for their children.

- The more education the children have, the more they are likely to engage in one or another form of continuing education throughout their lives. Education becomes more a part of life for more people in an accelerating fashion.

14 Postsecondary education is entering a new stage of life:

- Higher education will become a smaller component of expanding postsecondary education, and further education will become a larger segment of the total.

- The community college will become the most populous section of higher education and a connecting link with further education.

- Higher education will grow less in numbers of traditional students and more in numbers of nontraditional students.

- Higher education will confer less class status than it once did and less occupational advantage than it now does, but it will become more of a direct instrument for affecting the quality of life.

- College (the "Alma Mater") will become less important at any single moment of life even as more forms of education become more inter-twined with all of life.

- Postsecondary education will be even more torn among attention to *(a)* the academic, which first served the professions, and *(b)* the technical, which helped give rise more recently to the industrial meritocracy, and *(c)* the affective, which now caters more to certain members of an affluent society; between concentration on the campus, on the work place, and on leisure-time locations; between the preparation for life inherent in academic and technical training, and the experience of life inherent in the greater attention to the emotional and affective aspects of life.

- Higher education will face more political competition from further education. It will need to strengthen its connections with society. The state university campus that once stood alone and supreme in the affection of the people of the state now finds many more competitors on its flanks.

- The limits to what constitutes higher education may still be sufficiently clear-cut to warrant efforts at accreditation, but the limits to what constitutes some form of postsecondary education will be so very fuzzy that useful definitions for purposes of inclusion and exclusion will be difficult and sometimes impossible. It will still be possible to define a *student* in higher education but very difficult or even impossible to define a *student* in some areas of further education.

- A new direction of growth is developing. The first was the largely self-contained classical college beginning in 1636. The second was the society-related land-grant university after the Civil War. The third was universal access to college for the "college-age" group after World War II. The fourth, now developing, is universal access —even approaching universal attendance—for persons of all ages to more forms of postsecondary education.

15 Society is also entering a new stage:

- Where more people want more options among work, education, and leisure throughout their lives; more opportunities to assess possibilities and change directions; more extension of the potentialities of youth into age. The "optional" society is replacing one where people were more likely to be "tracked" for life; although there are, to be sure, counterefforts among some groups and individuals to perpetuate or to create one preferred life pattern.

- Where the "steady-state" environmental requirements of the future will mean that more people will need to engage in activities which are low consumers of energy and metals—education is one major possibility.

Postsecondary education has become more central to society and to the changes that take place within it.

16 The central messages of this report are these:

- That postsecondary education should be concerned comparatively less with the welfare of a minority of the young and more with that of a majority of all ages

- That more and better channels for all of youth should be created into life and work and service; for the one-half that do not now go to college as well as for the one-half that do go

- That age should be welcomed along with youth into the facilities for education; that continuing education, like libraries and museums, should be open to all ages; that the educational barriers separating the age groups be removed

- That education should help create an easier flow of life for all persons from one endeavor to another; that it be a more universal tool of leverage on the processes of life; that, in particular, the walls between work and education and leisure be torn down

- That postsecondary education take more forms; but that academic programs remain at the center of attention with the highest prestige and the greatest support

- That higher education concentrate on academic programs, leaving the quasi- and nonacademic programs largely to others; that it continue as the great source of scholarship and the pre-eminent leader in terms of high standards of effort

- That new policies, reflecting these goals, be developed on financing, accreditation, and coordination

- That the "learning society" can be a better society

2. The Totality of Postsecondary Education

In 1900, only 6 of each 100 persons 17 years old graduated from high school; by 1970, 75 of each 100 17-year-olds graduated from high school and 50 percent of the high school graduates went on to college. As the proportion of high school graduates attending college increased, those who did not go to college began to feel more sharply the economic and social handicaps of not having a college degree. This situation gave impetus to a national push for equality of educational opportunity and its implementation through universal access to college. Several factors made colleges and universities the principal original focus for universal access:

1 Colleges and universities have historically demonstrated their capacity to adapt to the nation's research, scientific, and professional needs, and it seems natural to expect them to adapt also to the new demands for universal access.

2 College attendance and college degrees are not only symbols of educational achievement, but also are important symbols of social status.

3 Research findings that college graduates enjoy higher earnings have been widely disseminated.

4 Many of the nation's employers give hiring preference to persons with college degrees—even when the jobs to be filled do not require college preparation.

5 Agencies of federal, state, and local governments provide either direct or indirect financial subsidies for colleges and universities that are generally unavailable to other postsecondary educational institutions.

6 Neither policy makers nor potential consumers have reliable information about effective alternatives to college attendance.

7 A few noncollegiate institutions that perform poorly have given good ones a bad reputation.

If these were the only factors to consider, college attendance could become as much the norm for youth as we move toward the twenty-first century as high school education was the norm by the mid-twentieth century. But, for many people, college is neither the only effective post-high school education option nor the best one:

1 Results of a 1969 study of student attitudes sponsored by the Carnegie Commission suggest that 1 out of every 10 students would prefer to be doing something other than going to college. An additional 2 out of every 10 students who indicated their disagreement with the statement, "I would rather be going to college than doing anything else" did so with reservations. Thus, of the 8 million students enrolled in 1969, somewhere between 800,000 and 2.4 million students would prefer not to be attending college.[1]

2 Colleges and universities, with the exception of their professional schools, quite properly regard job preparation as only one of their functions. For many college students, however, the primary motivation for attending college is to prepare for employment. Both the present oversupply of college graduates in the job market and several studies asserting a lack of relationship between college success and job performance or job satisfaction are reducing the attractiveness of college as a path to employment in some fields.

3 The widespread use by employers of degrees or diplomas as a prerequisite for employment is increasingly under attack. In the recent case of *Griggs v. Duke Power Company,* the court referred to the "infirmity of using diplomas or degrees as fixed measures of capability" and commented that "history is filled with examples of men and women who rendered highly effective performance without the conventional badges of accomplishment in terms of certificates, diplomas, or degrees" (401 *U.S. 424,* 91 *S. Ct. 849,* 28 *L. Ed. 2nd 158*).

4 Many of the nation's heaviest future manpower needs will be for skills which have not been taught in traditional college programs.

[1] See Carnegie Commission on Higher Education (1972, Table A-28, Appendix A, pp. 98–99).

Many colleges lack the appropriate human and physical resources for teaching such skills.

5 While most colleges have been primarily concerned with the cognitive development of their students, many students are interested in the affective domain and in personal growth and development. They find that service activities, travel, or work experience may be at least as effective as traditional colleges for this type of learning.

6 Higher education, with its tightly structured blocks of education leading to clearly designated terminal points (degrees), may not be the best vehicle to foster lifelong learning, which is an increasingly recognized requirement for present society.

7 The rising cost of college education and competing demands of other activities on public budgets, have led many to call for fresh and more careful consideration of the alternatives to college attendance for educational activities beyond the high school.

8 The public, motivated by recognition of a shift in manpower needs and the rising costs of higher education, has become increasingly concerned about the mismatch between needs of the economy and expenditures on education beyond high school. It has exerted pressure for new emphasis on vocational or "career" education in the allocation of funds.

As a result of these factors, the early 70s have witnessed a new interest in forms of education beyond high school which take place outside colleges and universities.

THE COMPONENTS OF POSTSECOND-ARY EDUCATION It is doubtful that any effort to list all postsecondary educational institutions and activities could be complete, but the following suggests the total range.

Postsecondary institutions

1 Colleges and universities (the Carnegie Commission classification of colleges and universities lists 18 subcategories of colleges and universities including two-year colleges and various types of specialized colleges)

2 Private trade, technical, and business schools (profit and nonprofit)

3 Correspondence schools

4 Area vocational schools

5 Public adult schools

Postsecondary education occurring outside postsecondary educational institutions

1 Educational programs in business and industry

2 Educational programs in government

3 Educational programs in the military

4 Educational aspects of service programs, such as Peace Corps and Vista

5 Educational activities in prisons

6 Apprenticeship programs

7 Museums

8 Libraries

9 Television and radio

10 Civic organizations

11 Community agencies, such as YMCA and YWCA

12 Churches

13 Trade and professional associations

Efforts to contrast higher education and the remainder of postsecondary education are complicated by the use of certain terms that suggest that postsecondary education that does not occur in colleges and universities is somehow less important, more remote, or of secondary status. In the federal government's statistical publications, for example, elementary and secondary schools and degree-granting colleges and universities are referred to as "regular" schools and postsecondary activities, are referred to as *peripheral regular.*" In the search for descriptive terminology, some writers refer to colleges and universities as *core* institutions, while other postsecondary institutions, such as private technical and business schools and postsecondary activities, are referred to as *peripheral.* (Moses, 1971, p. 2). The use of *core* and *peripheral* suggests that there is a single system with a single defined objective. But if there is a plurality of objectives, then presumably some institutions may be at the "core" for some objectives, while being on the "periphery" for others. Thus, Esalen could be considered a core institution if the designated educational objective is development of self-awareness, and the three Bryman Schools in California might be considered core institutions for purposes of training women for careers as paraprofessionals in medicine and dentistry. A four-year liberal arts college might be considered peripheral to both these limited purposes.

There is no question, however, that postsecondary education outside colleges and universities has, for public policy purposes, been treated as though it were peripheral. Competencies gained in activities of this kind are not given the same recognition as comparable competencies gained in two- and four-year colleges. But this differential treatment among postsecondary institutions becomes progressively harder to justify as both colleges and various special schools modify their programs in ways that blur intrinsic distinctions.

In the United States, since the mid-19th century, the meaning of the term *higher education* and the content of degree programs has been gradually expanded to incorporate much that would be considered *further education* or *vocational training* in other nations. This process was accelerated by four mid-20th century developments:

- The rapid expansion of two-year community colleges with their combination of general education and vocational training programs

- The move toward maximum student choice in the course content of a B.A. program

- The acceptance by college-degree holders of positions in occupations other than the prestigious professions

- The move toward granting degree credit for a great variety of off-campus experiences including employment and service activities

Today the distinctions between higher education programs and other postsecondary education seems to turn more on whether degree credit is awarded than on the intrinsic nature of the activity leading to credit. Even this distinction becomes somewhat artificial as some colleges begin to award college credit on a posthoc basis, and as the right to grant degrees is extended, at least under some circumstances, to private specialty schools and to rapidly developing new branches of existing institutions and to various new institutions, such as Empire State College in New York and Lincoln State University in Illinois, designed to grant special degrees tailored to individual student needs and circumstances (Benoit, 1973, pp. 422–425).

Although this process of amalgamation and incorporation is moving fairly rapidly, it is still possible to make some generalization concerning differences between education at colleges and universities and other postsecondary education.

If all types of postsecondary education institutions were arranged on a continuum ranging from those with highly limited educational purposes to those with multieducational purposes, colleges and universities would tend to cluster at the multipurpose end of the continuum (general education plus specialized, liberal education plus professional and career education, and personal emotional growth plus cognitive growth). Other postsecondary educational institutions are generally clustered at the highly limited educational purpose end of the continuum (narrowly defined occupational skills, specific leisure and recreational skills, specific cultural knowledge) (Chart 2).

If we shift the focus to the learner's purpose in participating in a postsecondary educational experience, we might utilize a continuum based on whether the learner is interested in educational consumption (either present consumption, in which the educational experience itself is the desired end, or deferred consumption, in which the learning is for future personal recreation or leisure goals) or for capital creation purposes (in which the educational goal is to develop some skill or knowledge for the purpose of producing income).[2] On this continuum, moving from consumption purposes to capital creation purposes, we find college and university education clustered toward the middle with a mixture of both purposes, while

[2] This might also be referred to as a pleasure-gain continuum.

CHART 2 *Postsecondary education: multipurpose and single purpose*

Multipurpose	*Single purpose*

←——→

Higher education	Further education
Universities	Military Specialty
Comprehensive colleges	programs schools
Community colleges	National and
Liberal arts colleges	service programs
	programs

CHART 3 *Postsecondary education: human capital creation and present and deferred consumption*

Human capital creation	*Both*	*Present and deferred consumption*

◄───►

Technical training	Higher education	Leisure activities
Experiential programs (in part)		Emotional adjustment programs
		Experiential programs (in part)

other postsecondary education tends to cluster at each of the extreme ends of the continuum (Chart 3).

Thus, many postsecondary learners look outside colleges and universities when their purpose is either almost purely for consumption (cultural education of museums, personal growth groups, educational activities for leisure), or, when their purpose is almost exclusively to create capital (computer program schools, business schools, cosmetology schools). Considered in this way, some postgraduate professional schools of universities might be considered more similar to institutions outside colleges and universities than to undergraduate colleges in which there is a greater mingling of consumption and capital creation purposes.

While, for some time, education at colleges and universities has been treated more favorably than other postsecondary education in public policy, the above two analyses suggest that this may not continue to be the case. Rising levels of public investment in colleges and universities have led to two important public concerns: (1) new measures of accountability and (2) relevance for manpower development. On both concerns, certain types of noncollege postsecondary institutions may fare better than colleges and universities. The new measures of accountability frequently call for demonstrations of the capacity of the institution to accomplish certain stated objectives. This type of accountability is far easier to achieve and demonstrate in institutions that have narrowly limited purposes than in multipurpose universities. Relevance for manpower development is also substantially easier to establish for institutions which are frankly and narrowly vocational in purpose than for colleges and universities with general education commitments. The public's willingness to extend student subsidies to learners at noncollegiate postsecondary institutions has thus far extended only

to students who are pursuing vocational programs. There are dan
gers that colleges and universities may overreact or react inappro
priately to these two public concerns, particularly the second, in
an effort to retain their favored position in the range of postsecond
ary education.

**LIFELONG
LEARNING**

Education generally calls to mind the passage of youth through
the schools into adulthood, a stage presumably reached somewhere
around age 18 or 21. The age of students is, itself, therefore re
garded as a distinguishing feature of certain types of institution:
of postsecondary education. Colleges and universities, for example
are popularly regarded as provinces of the young. But this view is
increasingly at odds with reality. Statistically and legally (even
ignoring that the age of majority has been lowered in many state:
since the passage of the 26th amendment to the Constitution of the
United States) *about 42 percent of all students on college and uni
versity campuses are adults.*

The presence of such large proportions of adults in the studen
bodies of colleges and universities calls into question the view tha
learning beyond the high school is solely a preparation for life. I
is, instead, a part of life itself—and as much so at a college or uni
versity as it is at other postsecondary institutions of education.

The concept of education as preparation for life is further chal
lenged by the fact that our world is constantly changing at an ever
quickening rate, so that the time is past when "a person could an
ticipate living his life in the world into which he was born" (Bergin
1971). In today's world, men and women need not only solid educa
tional foundations, but also lifelong opportunities to adapt, to renew
themselves, and to acquire new knowledge. And their lifelong ques
for such opportunities will lead them to the full spectrum of insti
tutions within postsecondary education.

Pursuit of this quest will be made increasingly easy by antici
pated changes in the conditions of people's lives. On the whole
these changes involve increasing freedom for nonwork activities
and from societal pressures that now restrict participation in edu
cation to certain times in one's life. Already there has been some re
laxation of society's expectations that young persons enter a college
or university immediately upon graduation from high school and
stay in student status without interruption until they have earned
their degrees. Combining studenthood with family responsibilities
is also much more common than it once was. Beyond these changes

Gösta Rehn, Director of Manpower and Social Affairs for the Organisation for Economic Co-operation and Development (OECD), perceives other trends in the economy of industrialized nations that will free schedules and funds for learning activities. Among them is a progressive reduction in total hours of work per lifetime accompanied by increasing levels of real income per hour—a combination that will allow for variations in the allocation of one's working time. He expects gradual reduction of weekly work hours to make part-time "moonlighting" possible, thus eroding the full-day work schedule generally. He expects that the secondary and tertiary educations that are increasingly available at low or no cost to youths in many countries will eventually be demanded by adult taxpayers as well. Expansion of the service sector of the economy, which easily provides employment for persons who want to have part-time work and irregular working schedules, will also alter our concepts of the normal working day. Urbanization will require varied and flexible arrangements for daily, weekly, and annual timing of work and leisure in order to reduce congestion. Finally, increasing numbers of persons in the labor force will have a particular need or a particular propensity for other than the ordinary patterns for working time. Among these will be women with family responsibilities, older workers in need of less strenuous work situations, and persons who have embraced new lifestyles that cannot be accommodated by rigidly enforced work roles (Rehn, 1972, pp. 14–17). Changes of the sort Rehn describes are, in fact, taking place in society now, and they will ultimately change normal assumptions Americans have about what they can and cannot do with their adult lives. Continuing or recurrent learning is an increasingly feasible option.

3. Participation in Postsecondary Education

MANY
PARTICIPATED
IN MANY
PROGRAMS As part of the Current Population Survey in May 1969, all persons 35 years old and over, and those 17 to 34 years of age who were not enrolled in regular school full time, were asked if they had participated in education and training activities during the previous year. An estimated 13.2 million Americans — 11.0 percent of the 119.7 million "eligible" adults — said that they had participated (USOE, 1971, pp. 11, 15).

Preliminary unpublished tabulations from a CPS survey taken in 1972 indicate that some 15.7 million persons, or approximately 12 percent of the "eligible" adult population, participated in adult education activities during the year immediately preceding.

The increases observed in the Current Population Survey reinforce the findings of other surveys carried out under private auspices.

The most recent private survey was conducted under the sponsorship of the Commission on Non-Traditional Study by the Response Analysis Corporation, in collaboration with the Western Office of the Educational Testing Service. For this study a representative sample of persons 18 to 60 years of age were surveyed in the summer of 1972, and as a result of this study it is estimated that 32.1 million out of approximately 104 million persons (30.9 percent) had received instruction within the preceding 12 months in a specified list of subject skills in "evening classes, extension courses, correspondence courses, on-the-job training, private lessons, independent study, T.V. courses or anything like that" but excluding subjects taken as a full-time student (Commission on Non-Traditional Study, 1973, p. 18).

On the basis of these surveys it is clear that the annual participation of adults in educational activities has grown. Whether it has grown as fast as Stanley Moses has estimated, however, is highly unlikely. Moses projected that in 1975 there would be 82.4 million adults enrolled in programs offered by "peripheral" sources (Moses, 1971).[1] The assumption is that most of those enrolled in such programs would be adults.

But annual participation is only one measure of adult learning. What is learned, the intensity and duration of learning efforts, and the extent to which the same people show up on statistics year after year are also important. From the evidence of the several surveys we looked at, we conclude that the average duration of sustained learning effort is considerably less than one year. In a survey undertaken by the National Opinion Research Center (NORC) in 1962, 77 percent of the respondents took a single course. The average number of courses was 1.32. Three-fourths of the participants studied in a single subject area (Johnstone & Rivera, 1965, p. 39). Taking a longer time span, approximately three-fifths of the adult population engage in relatively systematic adult learning activities beyond their formal schooling. As part of the NORC study, adults were asked: "Thinking back over the time since you left school, have you at any time since then taken an educational course of any sort—including things like evening classes, correspondence courses, lecture series, discussion groups, courses given over television, home studies, courses given by the armed services, or anything like that?" In response, 47 percent answered "yes." Another 38 percent—including some of those who also took courses—said they had ". . . tried to teach themselves some subject by means of independent study strictly on their own." All told, 61 percent reported having engaged in one form or another of adult learning ibid, p. 2).

The NORC study also identified vocational subject matter as the leading content of instruction—32 percent of all courses were in this area. Hobbies and recreation ranked second at 19 percent, followed by general education, religion, and home and family life at 12 percent each. Each of the four remaining categories—personal development, public affairs and current events, agriculture, and miscellaneous—accounted for less than 5 percent of the courses taken (ibid., 1965, p. 51).

In the study for the Commission on Non-Traditional Study, it was found that more persons (13.4 million) had tried to learn something about hobbies and recreation than about vocational subjects

[1] Identified as sources other than conventional schools, colleges, or universities.

TABLE 1
*Subject areas
studied by
adult learners*

Areas of learning	Number (in millions)	Percentage*
Vocational subjects (excluding agriculture)	11.2	35.0
Hobbies and recreation	13.4	41.8
General education	8.1	25.2
Home and family life	4.3	13.3
Personal development	3.7	11.4
Public affairs	2.1	6.4
Religious studies	4.4	13.8
Agriculture	1.1	3.4

* Percentages add to more than 100 because some persons engaged in more than one area of learning.

SOURCE: Adapted from Table 2 "Areas of Learning Indicated as the First Choice of Would-be Learners and Studied by Learners" in Commission on Non-Traditional Study (1973, p. 17).

(11.2 million). This change from 1962 cannot be accounted for with certainty, but it may reflect the availability of more leisure time or perhaps some change in cultural values. In a pattern quite similar to that in the NORC study, general education, religious studies, and home and family life followed in that order, with relatively low levels of participation in agriculture, personal development, and public affairs (see Table 1).

Of particular relevance to this report is the question of *where* adult learning takes place. In studies conducted for the Commission on Non-Traditional Study, 11 general sources of adult learning activity were identified. Among them, academic institutions (high schools and colleges) were the most frequently utilized source — by 7.4 million learners who constituted 22.9 percent of the sample. The next most frequently mentioned were industry and employers with 5.9 million learners. Private specialized (proprietary) and correspondence schools ranked seventh on the list with 1.7 million learners (see Table 2).

**EDUCATION
AND TRAINING
FOR WORK** Although we have repeatedly emphasized that training people for occupational performance is but one of many important functions of postsecondary education, many of the issues surrounding educational policy legitimately concern how best to serve new labor force entrants, as well as other workers who have continuing or recurrent education and training needs.

	Number of	
TABLE 2 *Sources of adult learning activity*	*learners*	*Percentage*
Sponsor	*(in millions)*	*of learners*
Academic institutions, such as high schools and colleges	7.4	22.9
Industry and employers	5.9	18.4
Self-study	5.4	16.9
Community organizations, such as YMCA	2.8	8.7
Religious institutions	2.0	6.3
Government agencies	1.8	5.5
Proprietary and correspondence schools	1.7	5.3
Private tutors	1.4	4.4
Museums, galleries, performing arts studios	0.7	2.3
Recreation and sports groups	0.7	2.3
Other organizations or no response	2.2	7.0

SOURCE: Commission on Non-Traditional Study (1973, p. 82).

Chart 4 shows some of the major "flows" into and out of school, labor force, and home. Traditionally, educational policy has focused on the rectangles at the top of the page and on the triangle in the upper left-hand corner which show the levels of the formal system of education.

The experience of those who do not complete high school   There is no question that failure to complete high school impairs one's chances for employment. In 1971, 16.4 percent of the 16- to 24-year-old white men and women in the labor force who had not completed high school were unemployed. By comparison, 8.1 percent of those unemployed had graduated from high school (Table 3). For members of racial minorities and for women, the percentages unemployed were higher for both high school graduates and dropouts, but those who had completed high school maintained an apparent advantage.

The experience of those who do not attend college   Among youth who complete high school but do not go on to college, the first channels through which they emerge into the work force are the various curricula at the secondary school level: college preparatory, vocational, commercial, and general. Radically different proportions of students from these curriculum groups typically go on to college:

	October		
	1969	*1970*	*1971*
Men			
School dropouts	11.2	21.4	16.4
High school graduates	6.7	12.0	8.4
Women			
School dropouts	19.8	21.8	21.3
High school graduates	8.4	11.2	9.4
White			
School dropouts	13.4	18.7	16.4
High school graduates	6.7	10.6	8.1
Negro and other races			
School dropouts	18.1	31.2	23.9
High school graduates	15.8	19.8	15.8

* Refers to 16- to 24-year-olds in 1971, to 16- to 21-year-olds in 1969 and 1970.
SOURCE: U.S. Bureau of Labor Statistics, "Employment of High School Graduates and Dropouts," Special Labor Force Report Nos. 121, 131, and 145 (reprinted from the *Monthly Labor Review,* August 1970, May 1971, and May 1972).

approximately 80 percent of the college prep group, but only 30 to 40 percent of the "generals" and only 15 to 25 percent of those from the vocational and commercial tracks (Grasso & Shea, 1973, p. 4). Chart 5 shows the proportion of young men 14–17 years of age enrolled in high school in October 1966 who reported that they were enrolled in each of these high school curricula. Since tracking decisions are often not made until the 10th or 11th grade, the proportion of high school graduates ready for jobs or higher education —that is, the college prep and vocational–commercial students— is doubtless understated by the exhibit on the left. The pie chart on the right reveals the 1969 distribution by curriculum of employed men 17 to 27 years old who had exactly 12 years of education. [2]

Perhaps reflecting a secular increase in the prevalence of formal occupational training outside regular schools, over three-fifths of out-of-school young white men with exactly 12 years of schooling and over two-fifths of their black counterparts reported by 1969 that they had received training beyond high school (Table 4). Since

[2] Since high school graduates in the military service were not included in the sample design three years earlier, the proportions are only approximately representative of *all* high school graduates.

CHART 4 *Estimated "flows" into and out of selected school and labor force positions, 1972 (estimates, exclusive of intrayear moves)*

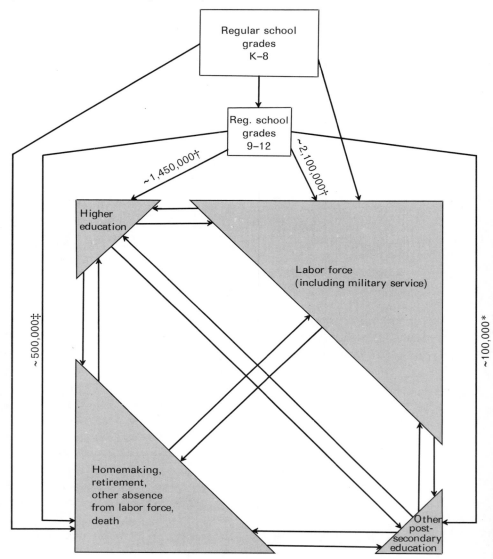

* Includes only persons not in labor force when surveyed in October CPS.

† Includes all persons who entered college in the fall from 1971–72 graduating class.

‡ Includes school dropouts and persons who enter military service.

NOTE: (1) Areas of rectangles and triangles are roughly proportionate to number of persons in each category at a moment in time.

(2) Figure ignores fact that many persons are in more than one category at any point in time.

SOURCE: Carnegie Commission Staff, 1973, based on USOE and Bureau of Census material.

TABLE 4 *Proportion of employed out-of-school young men 17–27 years of age with exactly 12 years of formal education who had some training beyond high school, and average duration of such training, by source of training, high school curriculum, and race*

Source of training	Vocational*		College prep		General	
	Percentage who received some training	Mean months of training received by those with some training	Percentage who received some training	Mean months of training received by those with some training	Percentage who received some training	Mean months of training received by those with some training
Whites						
Total, one or more sources†	62%	18	70%	16	58%	14
Business school or technical institute	16	14	22	11	22	12
Company school	21	9	25	9	15	7
Apprenticeship	9	28	8	26	8	17
Correspondence school	4	‡	13	9	6	9
Military training	18	14	17	11	22	7
Regular school (noncredit)	5	‡	9	‡	2	‡
Other	12	6	12	4	9	6
Blacks						
Total, one or more sources†	52%	8	53%	5	37%	10
Business school or technical institute	4	‡	6	‡	12	5
Company school	20	‡	12	‡	16	6
Apprenticeship	8	‡	0	‡	3	‡
Correspondence school	0	‡	0	‡	0	‡
Military training	16	‡	12	‡	10	‡
Regular school (noncredit)	0	‡	6	‡	1	‡
Other	16	‡	12	‡	8	‡

*Excludes commercial, not shown separately.

† Unduplicated percent; sum of percentages for each type may add to more than total because some men received training from more than one source.

‡ Not calculated; base less than 10 sample cases.

SOURCE: John T. Grasso and John R. Shea, "The Effects of High School Curriculum on Age-Earning Profiles," Center for Human Resource Research, the Ohio State University, (processed) 1972, Table 5.

CHART 5 *Approximate distribution of young men enrolled in school in 1966 and of high school graduates in October 1969, by curriculum in high school*

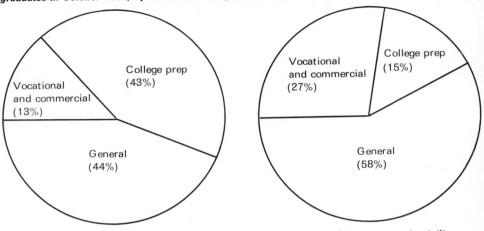

14- to 17-year-old young men who
were enrolled in high school,
October 1966

17- to 27-year-old young men in civilian
employment with exactly 12 years of
school completed, October 1969

SOURCE: Herbert S. Parnes, et al., *Career Thresholds*, vol. 1, Manpower Research Monograph No. 16, Government Printing Office, Washington, D.C., 1970, p. 26; John T. Grasso and John R. Shea, "The Effects of High School Curriculum on Age-Earnings Profiles," *Proceedings of the Social Statistics Section, American Statistical Association, 1972*, 1973.

there were a considerable number of veterans in the 14-to-24-year old civilian population in 1966, military training was a relatively common source of vocational skills. Company schools were impor- tant for both black and white employees, while business schools and technical institutes were patronized much more frequently by whites than blacks.[3] About 1 in 12 graduates reported apprentice training.

POST-
SECONDARY
EDUCATION
IN 1970

The staff of the Carnegie Commission has estimated that there were 74 million program enrollments in all postsecondary education and training activities in 1970 (Table 5). Because some people en- roll in more than one program during the year, however, the total number of persons enrolled is estimated at 57 million. If the degree- credit enrollment (8.9 million) is excluded, then 48 million persons —mainly adults—were engaged in postsecondary education and training activities. These estimates do not include participation

[3] Not only did relatively fewer black than white men receive postsecondary school training, but its average duration was considerably shorter—for ex- ample, 18 versus 8 months for those from the vocational track.

		Program enrollments		FTE enrollments	
	Source	Number* (thousands)	Percent¶	Number‡ (thousands)	Percent¶
	Total, higher education and other postsecondary education	73,800†	100.0	17,600	100.0
	Higher education				
	1. Colleges and universities (full-time degree credit)	8.900	12.1	8,900	50.6
	2. Colleges and universities (part-time degree-credit and non-degree credit)	6,300	8.5	1,950	11.1
	Other postsecondary education				
	1. Elementary and secondary schools	3,900	5.3	300	1.7
	2. Other public postsecondary programs	1,000	1.4	350	2.0
	3. Specialty schools				
	a. Proprietary (except correspondence)	3,800	5.1	1,350	7.7
	b. Correspondence schools	2,000	2.7	50	0.3
	4. Employers and associations (except armed forces)				
	a. Apprenticeships (registered)	400	0.5	100	0.6
	b. Apprenticeships (non-registered)	200	0.3	50	0.3
	c. Safety instruction	15,700	21.3	300	1.7
	d. Job orientation	7,400	10.0	550	3.1
	e. Other organized instruction	8,100	11.0	1,650	9.4
	5. Armed forces				
	a. Initial training	650	0.9	550	3.1

TABLE 5 *Estimated number of program enrollments and FTE enrollments beyond regular elementary and secondary education, by source, 1970*

		Program enrollments		FTE enrollments	
TABLE 5 *(continued)*	Source	*Number* (thousands)*	*Percent¶*	*Number‡ (thousands)*	*Percent¶*
	b. Correspondence	1,300	1.8	50	0.3
	c. Other organized instruction	1,100	1.5	850	4.8
6.	Prison	200	0.3	§	0.1
7.	Other government programs				
	a. Work Incentive Program, Job Corps, Neighborhood Youth Corps (out of school)	250	0.3	50	0.3
	b. Agricultural extension and other	500	0.7	50	0.3
8.	Unions	100	0.1	§	§
9.	Other government programs (e.g., TV, churches and synagogues. community organizations, libraries and museums, etc.)	10,000	13.6	400	2.3
10.	Tutors	2,000	2.7	100	0.6

* Estimated number of persons who participated at some time during the year; excludes informal learning at home, on the job, or elsewhere, and exclusively self-study.

† May overstate the number of separate persons by a factor of approximately 1.3 because of multiple program enrollments during the year.

‡ FTE is defined as 391 classroom hours, the estimated number of hours spent face-to-face in instructional setting by full-time degree-credit college students.

§ Less than 12,500, or less than 0.1 percent.

¶ Detail may not add to total because of rounding.

SOURCE: Carnegie Commission staff, 1973.

in self-study, independent study related to organized instruction, and informal learning activities at home, on the job, or elsewhere. Data on such activity is virtually impossible to obtain, especially on a large scale.

Judging the magnitude of postsecondary education by "head-count" enrollments alone can be misleading, however. Some of the learners thus counted are instructed for an hour or less a week while others pursue more time-consuming studies. Some take instruction of only a few weeks duration, while others may take it for a year or more. The demands of individual learners on institutional resources, therefore, vary significantly. For purposes of comparing the resource needs and effectiveness of the different types of postsecondary education programs, enrollments must therefore be converted into full-time-equivalent (FTE) enrollments. This conversion shrinks the numbers of nontraditional students. For example, 65 million nontraditional enrollments would be the equivalent (in hours) of having an additional 8.7 million full-time students in our colleges and universities at some time during the calendar year.

Colleges and universities accommodate about 12 percent of all program enrollments when a head-count measure is used (Table 5). But when program enrollments are translated into full-time equivalents, colleges and universities accommodate over three-fifths of the enrollment—51 percent in full-time degree-credit instruction and 11 percent of the part-time credit and non-degree-credit enrollment. If our interest is confined to nontraditional and further education, however, colleges and universities accommodate only 22 percent of the FTE enrollments.

Expenditures for various kinds of education and training are difficult to determine with precision. In traditional institutions, for which relatively good data is available, expenditures for student education (including a proportionate share of capital outlay) as opposed to organized research, other activities not related to educational purposes, auxiliary enterprise, student aid, and major public services, amounted to nearly $18 billion in 1970 (Table 6). Our data show that $15.4 billion was spent for full-time degree-credit instruction. This breaks down to about $4.44 per student manhour spent in instructional settings. By contrast, we estimate that some $13 billion was spent on education and training for adults and part-time students in colleges and other settings. Table 6 shows estimated costs for each source of training. In these tabulations, the instructional cost per program enrollment for higher education is $1,736 for full-time degree-credit students, an amount one-third again larger than that expended in any of the other pro-

	Number of program enrollments* (thousands)	Estimated cost of instructional services‡	
Source		Total (millions of dollars)	Percent
Total, higher and postsecondary education	73,800†	$28,453	100.0
Higher education			
1. Colleges and universities (full-time degree-credit)	8,900	15,412	54.2
2. Colleges and universities (part-time degree-credit and non-degree-credit)	6,300	2,282	8.0
Further education			
1. Elementary and secondary schools	3,900	289	1.0
2. Other public postsecondary programs	1,000	459	1.6
3. Specialty schools a. Proprietary (except correspondence)	3,800	1,610	5.7
b. Correspondence schools	2,000	263	0.9
4. Employers and associations (except armed forces) a. Apprenticeships (registered)	400	119	0.4
b. Apprenticeships (nonregistered)	200	38	0.1
c. Safety instruction	15,700	188	0.7
d. Job orientation	7,400	885	3.1
e. Other organized instruction	8,100	3,895	13.7
5. Armed forces a. Initial training	650	520	1.8
b. Correspondence	1,300	260	0.9
c. Other organized instruction	1,100	1,320	4.6
6. Prisons	200	46	0.2

TABLE 6 Estimated number of program enrollments and selected measures of costs associated with organized education and training beyond regular elementary and secondary education, by source, 1970

| Per program enrollment | Per enrollee manhour | Estimated value of forgone earnings or production (millions of dollars) | Estimated economic costs¶ | |
			Per program enrollment in 1970	Per enrollee manhour
$386	$4.13	$34,388	$852	$9.12
1,736	4.44	22,526	4,272	10.93
360	3.00	2,685	783	6.53
75	2.50	137	110	3.69
447	3.50	467	903	7.06
423	3.00	1,403	792	5.61
132	14.00	49	156	16.61
314	3.00	33	402	3.83
200	3.00	10	252	3.80
11	1.50	160	22	2.78
119	4.00	488	186	6.21
480	6.00	3,106	862	10.78
800	2.50	772	1,988	6.21
200	10.00	40	230	11.54
1,200	4.00	2,297	3,288	10.96
230	6.00	1	235	6.13

TABLE 6
(continued)

		Number of program enrollments* *(thousands)*	Estimated cost of instructional services‡	
Source			*Total (millions of dollars)*	*Percent*
Further education (continued)				
7.	*Other government programs*			
	a. *Work Incentive Program, Neighborhood Youth Corps, (out-of-school)*	250	$150	0.5
	b. *Agricultural extension and other*	500	75	0.3
8.	*Unions*	100	12	§
9.	*Other organized programs (e.g., TV, churches and synagogues, community organizations, libraries and museums, etc.)*	10,000	450	1.6
10.	*Tutors*	2,000	180	0.6

* Estimated number of persons who participated at some time during the year; excludes informal (i.e. unorganized) learning at home, on the job, or elsewhere, and exclusively self-study arrangements.

† May overstate the number of separate persons by a factor of approximately 1.3 because of multiple program enrollments during the year.

‡ Excludes value of forgone earnings (or production), shown separately. and incidental private educational costs (e.g., books and supplies); estimated enrollee manhours exclude independent study and homework related to instruction; per hour estimate refers to instructor-grader time devoted to each student in the case of correspondence and television instruction.

§ Less than 0.1 percent.

¶ Economic costs are defined as costs of instructional services plus forgone earnings (or production).

SOURCE: Carnegie Commission staff, 1973.

grams.[4] Adult and continuing education in colleges and universities cost only $360 per program enrollment. However, this is because much of it is offered for comparatively short periods of time. In order to present a picture of total economic costs, Table 6 includes estimates that include the forgone earnings of the typical participating students (or, where appropriate, the forgone produc-

[4] This average annual cost estimate is lower than conventional estimates because program enrollments in Table 6 include part-year as well as full-year students.

Per program enrollment	Per enrollee manhour	*Estimated value of forgone earnings or production (millions of dollars)*	*Estimated economic costs¶*	
			Per program enrollment in 1970	*Per enrollee manhour*
$600	$6.00	$ 23	$692	$6.92
150	5.00	12	174	5.80
120	4.00	6	180	6.00
45	3.00	118	57	3.79
90	6.00	55	117	7.83

tion of typical persons engaged in education rather than production in prisons or the military services). Calculated on this basis, the cost for each program enrollment in higher education is $4,272, about five times the average for all sources of education. The reason for the larger cost is again that enrollees in higher education spend virtually full time during most of the year in instruction and both their instructional costs and forgone earnings are correspondingly greater than those of persons engaged in programs offered by other sources.

The estimated cost of instructional services per enrollee manhour (Chart 6) is concentrated within a generally narrower range than is total economic cost per enrollee manhour (Chart 7), because the latter includes forgone earnings which vary from very little to substantial sums, depending on setting, program flexibility, number of weeks spent in the program, and other factors.

CHART 6 *Estimated cost of instruction per enrolee manhour in 1970, by source of postsecondary education*

Dollars per manhour

Source	
	$0 $5.00 $10.00 $15.00
Correspondence schools	$14
Correspondence (armed forces)	$10.00
Prisons	$6.00
National manpower programs	$6.00
Other organized instruction (employers and associations)	$6.00
Tutors	$6.00
Agricultural extension	$5.00
Colleges and universities (full-time degree credit)	$4.44
Average, all postsecondary education	$4.13
Job orientation	$4.00
Other organized instruction (armed forces)	$4.00
Unions	$4.00
Other public postsecondary programs	$3.50
Colleges and universities (part-time and non-degree-credit)	$3.00
Private specialty schools	$3.00
Apprenticeships (registered)	$3.00
Apprenticeships (nonregistered)	$3.00
Elementary and secondary schools	$2.50
Armed forces initial training	$2.50
Safety instruction	$1.50

Average, all postsecondary education

Higher education

SOURCE: Table 6.

PATTERNS OF POST- SECONDARY EDUCATION AND TRAINING TO 1980   Many factors will influence the future course of postsecondary education. Among them are (1) characteristics of the environment (for example, work and home life) that encourage learning activity; (2) opportunities (for example, time) for learning; (3) the presence or absence of attractive competing uses of time; (4) the expected "pay off"—both monetary and nonmonetary—to learning activity; (5) how adept different persons are at learning; (6) the effectiveness and efficiency with which potential sources of learning respond

CHART 7 *Estimated economic cost, including forgone earnings, per enrollee manhour, 1970, by source of postsecondary education*

Source	Dollars per manhour
Correspondence schools	$16.61
Correspondence schools (armed forces)	$11.54
Other organized instruction (armed forces)	$10.96
Colleges and universities (full-time degree-credit)	$10.93
Other organized instruction (employers and associations)	$10.78
Average, all postsecondary education	$9.12
Tutors	$7.83
Other public postsecondary programs	$7.06
Government manpower programs	$6.92
Colleges and universities (part-time and non-degree credit)	$6.53
Job orientation	$6.21
Armed forces (initial training)	$6.21
Prisons	$6.13
Unions	$6.00
Agricultural extension and other government programs	$5.80
Private specialty schools	$5.61
Apprenticeships (registered)	$3.83
Apprenticeships (nonregistered)	$3.80
Other organized programs	$3.79
Elementary and secondary schools	$3.69
Safety instruction	$2.78

Average all postsecondary education

Higher education

SOURCE: Table 7.

to learning needs; and (7) methods of financing postsecondary learning.

As indicated earlier in this report, futurists have identified several trends that should encourage lifelong learning activities. Not the least of them is the constant and rapid change to which our society is subjected, and to which people must respond by acquiring new skills and knowledge. Opportunities should increase as incomes rise, as shorter working hours and early retirements become more common, and as provision is made to provide financial support for persons who wish to seek postsecondary education at any time during their lives. "Pay offs" will remain high as long as our society rewards those who have acquired knowledge and related competencies.

Adult learning activity will increase generally in the years to come. For one thing, the educational attainment of our population is increasing, and a strong positive relationship has been found between participation in adult education and the highest year of school completed. For example, Johnstone and Rivera found that in measuring adult learning activity during 12 months immediately preceding June 30, 1962, fewer than 10 percent of persons with less than nine years of education were receiving some form of training, but 15 percent of those with exactly 12 years of schooling and more than a third of those with at least one year of college were active in educational endeavors (Johnstone & Rivera, 1965, p. 76). The more recent ETS–Response Analysis Corporation survey for the Commission on Non-Traditional Studies revealed a similar pattern.

In Chart 8 a consistent increase in levels of educational attainment of 25- to 29-year-olds in the American population is projected between 1940 and the year 2000—whether enrollments rise as rapidly as projected by the Commission in 1971 or more slowly as projected according to data available in 1973.

Studies also indicate that younger adults are more likely to participate in adult learning activities than older ones (USOE, 1959, p. 5; USOE, 1969, p. 11). In the NORC survey, the highest activity rate was reported by 20- to 29-year-olds (29.9 percent) and, once again, lowest for those at the oldest extreme of the scale (Johnstone & Rivera, 1965, p. 73). U.S. Bureau of the Census reported 30.9 million persons in the United States who were within the highest education participation age level reported by Johnstone and Rivera. By 1980, the number will exceed 40 million (U.S. Bureau of the Census, 1971, pp. 13–14).

In sum, because of both increasing educational attainment and increasing numbers of persons in the population who are in the educationally active young-adult age groups, we will have increasing numbers of adult learning participants for some time to come.

Because of the many uncertainties, however, it is difficult to estimate the future enrollments in postsecondary education. We have elsewhere (*New Students and New Places,* 1971*b*) estimated enrollments in higher education but have revised these projections

CHART 8 *Projected levels of educational attainment of the population 25 to 29 years of age*

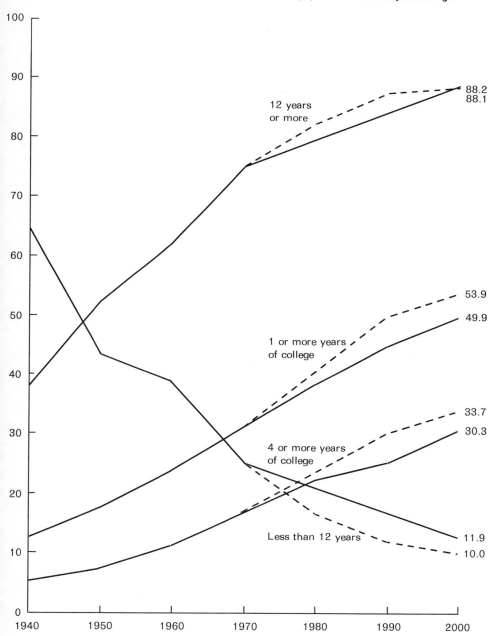

NOTE: Broken lines are based on assumptions consistent with Projection 1 prepared for the Carnegie Commission by Gus W. Haggstrom in 1971. Solid lines are based on assumptions consistent with Projection II prepared by the Carnegie Commission staff in 1973. Details of the later projections will appear in the Commission's forthcoming final report, *Priorities for Action.*

SOURCE: Carnegie Commission staff, 1973, based on Bureau of the Census and Carnegie Commission materials and assumptions.

for a subsequent report *(Priorities for Action)*. Generally, we expect full-time degree-credit enrollments to fall below earlier estimates, with part-time degree-credit and non-degree-credit enrollments continuing to rise at relatively high rates. It is even more difficult to estimate enrollments in further education. We do expect, however, for reasons given earlier, that these enrollments will, on the whole, rise faster than full-time degree-credit enrollments within higher education. Our estimates and percentage changes from 1970 to 1980 are shown in Table 7 and Chart 9.

TABLE 7
Estimated and projected number of program enrollments beyond regular elementary and secondary education, by source, 1970–80* (numbers in thousands)

Source	1970	1980	Percentage change, 1970–80
Total, regular and adults†	73,800	108,200	47
Higher education			
1. Colleges and universities (full-time degree credit)	8,900	11,500	29
2. Colleges and universities (part-time degree credit and non-degree credit)	6,300	9,800	56
Further education			
1. Elementary and secondary schools	3,900	9,000	131
2. Other public postsecondary programs	1,000	2,500	150
3. Specialty schools			
a. Proprietary (except correspondence)	3,800	8,000	111
b. Correspondence schools	2,000	3,500	75
4. Employers and associations (except armed forces)			
a. Apprenticeships (registered)	400	600	50
b. Apprenticeships (nonregistered)	200	300	50
c. Safety instruction	15,700	17,000	8
d. Job orientation	7,400	9,000	22
e. Other organized instruction	8,100	14,000	73
5. Armed forces			
a. Initial training	650	600	−8
b. Correspondence	1,300	1,300	0
c. Other organized instruction	1,100	1,400	27
6. Prisons	200	200	0

TABLE 7
(continued)

Source	1970	1980	Percentage change, 1970–80
7. *Other government programs*			
a. *Work Incentive Program, Job Corps, Neighborhood Youth Corps (out-of-school)*	250	350	40
b. *Agricultural extension and other*	500	500	0
8. *Unions*	100	150	50
9. *Other organized programs (e.g., TV, churches and synagogues, community organizations, libraries and museums, etc.)*	10,000	15,000	50
10. *Tutors*	2,000	3,500	75

* Estimated number of persons who participated at some time during the year; excludes informal (i.e., unorganized) learning at home, on the job, or elsewhere, and exclusively self-study arrangements.

† May overstate the number of separate persons by a factor of approximately 1.3 because of multiple program enrollments during the year.

SOURCE: Carnegie Commission staff, 1973.

CHART 9 *Estimated percentage changes in program enrollments, 1970 to 1980, in postsecondary education, by source*

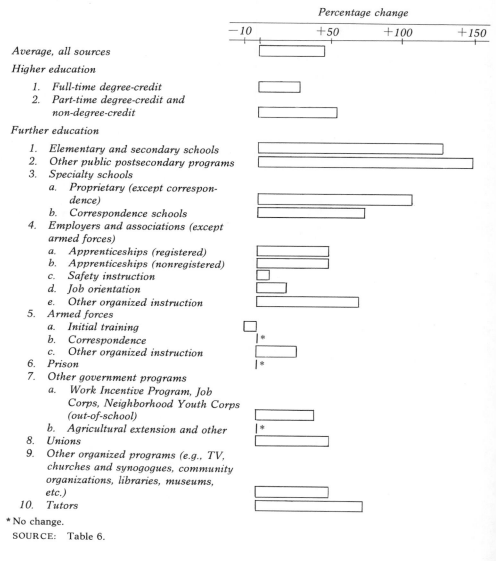

Percentage change

	−10	+50	+100	+150

Average, all sources

Higher education

1. Full-time degree-credit
2. Part-time degree-credit and non-degree-credit

Further education

1. Elementary and secondary schools
2. Other public postsecondary programs
3. Specialty schools
   a. Proprietary (except correspondence)
   b. Correspondence schools
4. Employers and associations (except armed forces)
   a. Apprenticeships (registered)
   b. Apprenticeships (nonregistered)
   c. Safety instruction
   d. Job orientation
   e. Other organized instruction
5. Armed forces
   a. Initial training
   b. Correspondence
   c. Other organized instruction
6. Prison
7. Other government programs
   a. Work Incentive Program, Job Corps, Neighborhood Youth Corps (out-of-school)
   b. Agricultural extension and other
8. Unions
9. Other organized programs (e.g., TV, churches and synogogues, community organizations, libraries, museums, etc.)
10. Tutors

* No change.

SOURCE: Table 6.

4. New Funding for Postsecondary Education

Higher education forms of postsecondary degree-credit instruction have increasingly become a public matter—three-fourths of all prebaccalaureate students are in public colleges and universities. Most further education forms of postsecondary education, on the other hand, have, until recently, been privately sponsored—for example, by private specialty schools, business firms, associations, and churches. Increasingly, however, public attention is being directed toward career education, mid-career retraining, continuing education for adults, and special programs for late entrants to the work force. The reports of the Commission on Non-Traditional Study (1973), Notre Dame's Study on Continuing Education (1973) and the Carnegie Commission (*Less Time, More Options,* 1971*a*) are evidences of a new interest in providing more educational alternatives to both youth and adults than have commonly been available.

An additional factor is the emergence of a new governmental philosophy of direct aid to students. For the past century or so, the public responsibility has been expressed primarily in the form of support for institutions under public control. Thus, in 1971–72 approximately 80 percent of public support of higher education was in the form of institutional subsidies. The trend in the last quarter of the twentieth century, however, is likely to be in the direction of supporting students and giving them greater latitude of choice as to where and in what form they pursue postsecondary education.

Dresch (1973) has argued that by primarily subsidizing institutions, "existing public (and private) policies have served to preclude the adaptive evolution of the postsecondary educational system." He views higher education as having become more standardized over the years, and argues that "effectively, the function of public policy has been to so heavily subsidize the dominant mode of educational delivery as to render alternatives nonviable." While developments in the community college sector over the last decade partially belie this, it is true that as far as public financial support is concerned, a sharp dividing line has been drawn between accredited nonprofit collegial institutions and other agencies offering postsecondary educational programs. This line has only just begun to be eroded by federal, state, and judicial action.[1]

In contemplating the financing of educational opportunities beyond the high school, one could argue that an ideal system should make it possible for one to undertake further education and training at the time(s) when it can most effectively aid one's career and development. For many persons, the period immediately succeeding high school may not be the most effective time—because of career indecision, immaturity, lack of motivation, alternative interests, or family responsibilities.

An optimal system also ought to help individuals add to their education and skill development periodically throughout their lives as they perceive new needs and wish to expand their horizons. This continuous learning process occurs in any event as the result of work or life experiences, but formal education can play a critical role in helping an individual to capitalize on emerging opportunities and interests.

For the last several decades in our society, most individuals' lives have been divided into three clearly delineated segments: up to age 21 one's time and energies were predominantly devoted to formal education (age 18 for the non-college attender; perhaps 25 or so for those who pursue an advanced degree); from 21 to 65 was the work period in one's life; the post-65 period has become principally devoted to retired leisure. Yet, ideally, learning, work, and leisure are part of a continuum stretching throughout the adult years.

For employed members of the labor force, the chief obstacles to pursuing education in later life are lack of time and financing. Anything other than an occasional evening course usually requires time away from one's job, and, except in the infrequent case where an employer arranges for and finances further education for em-

---

[1] Proprietary schools are now eligible for participation in many federal and state educational support programs, and the Higher Education Amendments of 1972, if fully implemented, would require representation on state planning agencies from sectors outside accredited institutions of higher education.

ployees, time away from work ordinarily involves a significant financial sacrifice.

The academic community is an occupational rarity in that it has long recognized the need for "sabbaticals"—paid educational leaves for scholarly purposes. In expanding fields of knowledge, intellectual obsolescence is recognized as a problem, and, in scholarly endeavors, recurring periods of concentrated re-education (ordinarily self-education) are commonly accepted as necessary. However, by the nature of the educational process, in terms of the formal work assignment of the college professor there is almost perfect substitutability. Thus the college or university, with adequate advance notice, can temporarily replace a teacher with little or no sacrifice in its educational services.

In government, commerce, or industry, such substitutability is less common; work processes are often more interdependent, or are part of a hierarchical chain of command. Thus an employer is less likely to encourage, or be indifferent to, repeated leaves of absence unless the long-range benefit to the enterprise is demonstrable. (Such benefits are most clearly present in the case of research workers, or in middle- and upper-level management echelons, and these are the areas where employers most frequently encourage further education of their staff.)

Yet, in an increasingly technological age, the personal benefits of intermittent education and training are high and rising. Combating skill obsolescence, easing labor force re-entry problems, career advancement, and the expansion of one's intellectual and cultural horizons are compelling reasons for individual pursuit of further education in one's adult years.

As in the case of the gradual shortening of the work week over the last century, however, it is difficult for employers to adjust the work process to individual preferences. Collective action will probably be necessary if the opportunities for recurrent education are to be made available to the adult population at large. This could occur in firms or industries through collective bargaining, or—as is now occurring in several Western European countries—a societal mandate through legislative action might establish a common procedure for educational leaves of absence.

THE MARKET FOR ADULT EDUCATION   The educational attainment of the adult population in the United States has continuously improved over the last century. In 1959 the median years of school completed by members of the civilian labor force finally reached 12 years, and by 1972 was approximately 12.5. But, while high school completion is now experienced by about three-fourths of the young, a considerable segment of the population has had insufficient education to reach their full work potential. As Table 8 indicates, only 27.5 percent of the civilian labor force have completed one or more years of college; 31.9 percent have not completed high school; 15.2 percent have had no secondary schooling. Thus, among the 72.5 percent who have not attended college, and the additional 13.9 percent who have had less than four years of college, there is a considerable potential demand for adult postsecondary education.

Three general types of recurrent education which are somewhat different in nature and with which one associates somewhat different problems might be identified. One type is *general education,* which includes some students who are part-time degree-credit students attempting to complete a course of study at the associate and baccalaureate level and perhaps an equal number who are enrolled in non-degree programs of a cultural or recreational nature. The latter group of adult students would ordinarily engage in such studies on a part-time basis in any event, and, except for the problem of meeting tuition costs. by and large they present no major problem of financing. The former group, however, in most instances would prefer to pursue full-time study, and a large proportion of them are prevented from doing so by the difficulties of obtaining leave from employment and compensating for lost earnings while engaging in further studies.

The second identifiable category of recurrent education is *vocational* in nature. A large number of such students are enrolled in instruction offered by business and industry and the armed forces. A still larger group, almost 1.4 million (Table 5), are enrolled in proprietary schools, and about 650,000 are scattered

TABLE 8
Percent of civilian labor force 18 years and older who have completed various lengths of schooling, 1971

	Male	Female	Both sexes
Less than 5 years	2.7%	1.4%	1.7%
5 to 8 years	15.8	11.5	13.5
9 to 11 years	16.9	16.4	16.7
High school graduation	35.7	45.4	39.4
1 to 3 years of college	14.0	13.9	13.9
4 or more years of college	14.9	11.4	13.6

SOURCE: *U.S. Department of Labor,* March 1972, Table B-9.

among correspondence schools, church and civic organization programs, and general programs such as agricultural extension, Job Corps, and Vista. The major proportion of these adult students are participating on a part-time basis. It seems likely that the largest potential demand for both full- and part-time study is in this area. While employer-sponsored programs generally provide for continuing compensation of the employee, the monetary cost and forgone income involved in further study is the greatest barrier for those participating in nonemployer programs.

The third category is what might be called *professional*—further training or refresher education for persons in middle- and upper-management levels, for research personnel, or for professional workers in health, legal, accountancy, public administration, and other similar employment. Income maintenance problems present the greatest barrier to this category of persons.

In light of the somewhat different problems faced by these three categories (and sub-categories) of adult students, it may be appropriate to treat the tuition and income maintenance issues separately. Forgone income is the primary obstacle to further study on the part of employed members of the labor force, while tuition costs are often the most immediate problem faced by the housewife or inactive member of the potential labor force. About one-half of the FTE adults in postsecondary education may be said to encounter one or the other or both of these problems.

TUITION COSTS AS A BARRIER TO POST-SECONDARY EDUCATION

Tuition costs are a recognizable barrier to attendance at college, and higher educational institutions, as well as federal and state student-aid programs, have attempted to alleviate this problem for the student from a low-income family. The Higher Education Amendments of 1972 also extend recognition to private specialty schools, and many additional students are now eligible for participation in federal assistance programs.

Either through low subsidized tuitions in public institutions or through student aid, the problem of meeting tuition charges on the part of low-income students is moderately well-met today. In 1971–72 approximately $4 billion in student assistance funds (not including loans, but including veterans' educational benefits) was expended by institutions, governments, and philanthropic agencies. Total tuition charges for the universe of higher education in that year were $5.5 billion. While at first glance this may seem to be an adequate balance, total subsistence costs for students in college amounted to approximately $7 billion. Thus only about 32 percent of direct monetary outlays were covered by student assistance.[2] In addition, many forms of student assistance (most notably benefits under the GI Bill, where the basis of allocation is past public service rather than current need) currently are not distributed strictly on the basis of need. and so student assistance funds are not maximally effective in aiding the needy.

Adult students who no longer receive parental aid frequently find the tuition barrier more imposing and scholarship programs less well-adapted to their needs than younger students. In addition, tuition policies in public institutions often penalize the adult student. Traditionally, most extension and continuing education programs have been less well-subsidized than have degree-credit undergraduate programs; in many state colleges and universities, continuing education is priced to be self-supporting. For older students who have already taken advantage of subsidized under-graduate education, a reasonable argument can be made that they should shoulder a larger share of the real cost for further education. Many adult students, however, for one reason or another missed the opportunity to pursue postsecondary education immediately after high school. and under current policies lose the opportunity for a lifetime.

In an earlier report, the Carnegie Commission urged the development of a lifetime educational credit concept, whereby each person reaching age 18 would be assured of at least two years of post-secondary education subsidized by public funds at some time in his or her life. A "two years in the bank" drawing right was proposed (Carnegie Commission, 1971a) usable at any time in one's life. The low-tuition, two-year community college was considered the basic component in a system that assured this minimum provision.

Since the initial Carnegie Commission proposal, two new factors have arisen and require a somewhat broader context in which to consider the drawing-right concept. First, noncollegiate institutions (principally private specialty schools) are now eligible for participation in student assistance under various federal programs, and it is more commonly accepted that in certain areas of vocational training such institutions perform a valuable service that may

[2] See Carnegie Commission on Higher Education (1973) for an extended analysis of family costs.

not be duplicated in public campus institutions. And, second, the current trend appears to be in the direction of higher tuitions in public institutions and more substantial student assistance for the needy. The Basic Opportunity Grants program under the Higher Education Amendments of 1972, which, when fully funded, would provide up to half the cost of college attendance (maximum award of $1,400) for the student with full need, signals the assumption by the federal government of responsibility for basic funding of low-income students. The Carnegie Commission in *Higher Education: Who Pays? Who Benefits? Who Should Pay?* (1973) recently recommended an expansion of federal student aid and a gradual increase in tuition charges in public institutions until they reach approximately one-third of educational costs. If these developments occur, then tuition charges may become an even more substantial obstacle for the adult student unless some more formal means of providing a lifetime educational credit can be established.

It would be possible for an individual state to adopt a program whereby, for example, every resident was assured of a tuition credit for two years of postsecondary education usable at any time in his or her life. With a highly mobile population, however, it would be difficult to monitor such a program. It is also doubtful that the courts would uphold a plan which required a substantial residency requirement either preceding or subsequent to a period of education financed by a state tuition credit. Conceivably, such a credit could be made in the form of a loan, with, say, one-fifth of the loan principal to be canceled for each year that one filed (or was claimed as a dependent on) a state income tax return.

In a recently suggested alternative approach (see Cartter, 1973) the federal government would undertake to make such a tuition credit available. Under this plan. the federal government would provide half tuition credit for up to four years of postsecondary education (the equivalent of "two years in the bank"), with perhaps a maximum award of $1,500. As an offset, the elimination of income tax deductions for educational expenses and over-18 dependent's allowances, elimination of social security dependent's allowances for over-18 children in college, and reduction of GI Bill benefits by an amount corresponding to the tuition grant is proposed. These adjustments would save the federal treasury about $2.5 billion today, which would be approximately the annual cost of the half-tuition credits. Administered through the social security administration, the monitoring problem would be negligible, and such drawing rights could be used sequentially or periodically at any age.

If such a plan were in effect, perhaps supplemented by a liberal income-contingent loan program, such as we have elsewhere proposed, and by other scholarship programs for those with demonstrated need, and if students were free to attend public, private, or proprietary institutions, it would appear that greater equity among individuals would be provided over time. The man or woman who did not pursue postsecondary education at 18, but who wished to do so at 28 or 40, perhaps in a non-degree program or in a vocational program in a proprietary school, would not be unduly penalized. Two-thirds of state and federal taxes from which educational subsidies now come are paid by persons who do not directly benefit from that support—such taxpayers are either non-college-attenders or go to independent colleges and universities. Particularly for those who missed college altogether when they were young, providing the opportunity later in life to improve their education and skills would seem to be an important societal responsibility.

PAID EDUCATIONAL LEAVE The majority of adults who might engage in further studies are employed members of the labor force, and for anything more than periodic out-of-hours, part-time study such persons must be able to get full- or part-time leave of absence and have some offset to lost earnings while engaged in study. Paid educational leave of absence is an unusual practice in the United States and is found mainly in large corporations for middle management and research personnel or in federal government service. In many countries, however, significant major steps have been taken in this direction over the last few years.

The most notable case is France, where under the Continuing Vocational Education Act of 1971 an employer-employee payroll tax (initially set at 0.8 percent each, but rising to 2 percent by 1976) provides income maintenance funds for workers participating in approved vocational education programs. These may be company-sponsored or external programs approved by employer-employee industrial councils. Participants receive at least 90 percent of the current average wage for their occupational grouping, and approved programs may be up to one year in length if full-time, or up to 1,200 hours for part-time instruction. In the initial years, approximately 2½ percent of the labor force of large companies may be on leave at any one time. As the International Labour Organisation report (1972) on paid educational leave notes:

The new Act establishes the principle of continuing vocational training as an integral part of lifelong education, such training consisting of initial and further training for adults and young persons who are in, or about to enter, employment. Its stated purpose is to enable workers to adapt to changes in techniques and in conditions of work and to promote their social advancement and participation in cultural, economic, and social development (1972, p. 9).

Somewhat less comprehensive programs of paid educational leave are in force in other industrial countries. In the United Kingdom, under the Industrial Training Act of 1964, industrial training boards have been created in 29 major industry groupings to encourage occupational training. Although the act does not mandate a leave program, the board is empowered to impose a levy on employers and to make grants and loans covering maintenance and travel for participants in approved programs. "Sandwich" course programs and on-the-job training are principally assisted by the boards.

Paid educational leave in the USSR is provided for under Act No. 2-VIII of the Supreme Soviet (1970). Both manual and nonmanual labor are encouraged to participate in work-study industrial training programs. In addition, paid leaves of absence for further study on the part of managerial, technical, and scientific personnel has been a practice in the Soviet Union since 1959. Romania, Poland, and Czechoslovakia have somewhat similar continuing vocational training programs for industrial and governmental employees.

In the Federal Republic of Germany, paid educational leave programs cover many categories of civil servants at the federal, state, and local levels. In 1969 several acts further encouraged (but did not establish as a right) leave programs for education leading to occupational advancement. Limited programs exist in Denmark, Norway, Sweden, and Belgium under governmental auspices.

In several countries, paid educational leave has become a common feature in collective agreements. This is fairly common in both France and Italy. In Great Britain about 4 million workers are covered by such arrangements, although most of these agreements are limited to young workers and apprenticeship programs.

Managerial and technical training programs are commonly found in the United States, and the practice has become more popular in Western Europe over the last several years. The American practice has been principally to grant fellowships for participation in university-administered programs, although in a number of cases educational institutes (or, as in the case of General Motors, even degree programs) are run by the companies themselves or by industry or management associations.

There has been considerable growth in similar types of high-level training programs over the last five years, involving the continuation of salary while engaged in further study in Germany, France, Belgium, and the United Kingdom.

Thus the concept of paid educational leave is no longer a rarity, and several nations are considering following the lead of France in establishing it as a right for all members of the work force—or even the entire adult population. In 1965, the International Labour Organisation adopted a resolution advocating "the access of workers to various types of paid educational leave, as distinct from holidays with pay for recreational purposes, in order to give them the opportunity and incentive to acquire the further education and training which they need to carry out their duties at the workplace and to assume their responsibilities as members of the community" (1972, p. 1).

As one analyzes the economic and technological history of modern society, the movement toward recurrent lifetime education with adequate provision to offset personal income loss appears to be a logical step for the last quarter of the twentieth century. Particularly in the United States, where universal access to collegiate education is now nearly assured to all youth, the next step in the evolution of our educational system would seem to be the assurance that lifetime educational opportunities be within reach of all motivated adults.

The problem of income maintenance, however, remains the single major obstacle; until some means can be found to ease the financial burden on aspiring individuals the principle of lifelong education will remain largely a dream.

ALTERNATIVE MAINTENANCE-OF-INCOME PROPOSALS Various alternatives exist for offsetting income loss while an adult member of the labor force participates in recurrent education. These alternatives might be categorized as coming under public or private sponsorship and as being contributory or noncontributory, and if contributory, being voluntary or compulsory.

Privately funded programs are either of an individual or collective nature. In the former case the student assumes the responsibility for a shift of lifetime resources from earning periods to periods of leave of absence for educational purposes. While this is commonly done in the case of the student who draws on private savings while undergoing further education, the principal external source of assistance is through loan programs. Loans, whether conventional ·or with variable repayment rates, are a means of deferring tuition or other educational expenses, and may be thought of as being voluntary and contributory.

Collective agreements between unions and employers with paid educational leave provisions are rather uncommon in the United States at present, but are frequently found in Italy and France. Such arrangements are ordinarily noncontributory (except insofar as one might argue that the incidence of employer-provided fringe benefits is really upon the wage earner) and include all workers under contract. In the event that no publicly administered program emerges in the United States over the next few years, it seems likely that paid leave-of-absence provisions will become a more common feature of contract negotiations in the future.

Publicly funded programs, except for sabbaticals for teachers in public colleges and universities and provisions in some federal and state agencies for job-related further education, are nonexistent in the United States. However, there have been a variety of proposals over the last several years for federally sponsored programs. Four of them illustrate possible approaches to the problem of providing maintenance of income during periods of educational leave.

1   In an article in the *New Republic* in 1969, James Tobin and Leonard Ross outlined a proposal for a National Youth Endowment:

At age 18, every youth in the nation—whatever the economic means of his parents or his earlier education—would have available from the federal government a line of credit or "endowment" of, for example, $5,000. A young man or woman could draw on this "National Youth Endowment" for authorized purposes until his twenty-eighth birthday (extensions of time could be allowed for military service or periods of social service like Peace Corps or VISTA). Authorized purposes would include not merely academic higher education, but also vocational schooling, apprenticeship, and other forms of accredited on-the-job training.

For every dollar used, the individual would assume liability for payment of extra federal income tax after he reaches age 28 (or as extended). The terms of this repayment (for example, one percent of income per $3,000 borrowed) would be set so that the average individual would, over his lifetime, repay the fund in full, plus interest at the government's borrowing rate. However, the government might decide to set less stringent terms and to subsidize the endowment, using the loan program as a vehicle for general support of education beyond high school.

A Youth Endowment program would leave the choice of schooling entirely up to the student. Borrowers could pick freely among public and private institutions (including profit-making vocational schools), rather than having to tailor their training to the changing contours of government aid programs. Their choices would redress the unbalanced emphasis that has characterized government assistance (long on support for the sciences, for academically gifted students and universities, and for experimental training programs for the hard-core unemployed; shorter shrift for the average American's 2.4 children).

Preliminary estimates of repayment terms needed for a program covering only academic education suggest that a surcharge of 1/3 of one percent of income per $1,000 borrowed would suffice. Broadening the proposal to include vocational students would raise the required surcharge, and the rate would jump further if students with high income prospects disdained to participate. To hold this clientele, the program might include a feature allowing a borrower to avoid further surcharges once he has repaid the loan at a specified and abnormally high interest rate.[3]

The Tobin-Ross proposal, while designed primarily for young adults (up to age 28) and aimed primarily at meeting tuition costs, could — with some liberalizing of age and loan ceilings — provide living costs while a student was engaged in study. Basically it is a voluntary loan program, with repayment risks shared by all participants, rather like the Educational Opportunity Bank proposed by the Zaccharias Committee, using the federal income tax as a repayment mechanism.

2   Stephen Dresch, in a paper presented at the Georgetown University Conference on Recurrent Education in 1973, expanded on the Tobin-Ross plan, and proposed a Human Investment Fund, designed more for the adult student. Under his proposal:

The endowment would become available at age 18, with a maximum value of perhaps, $10,000. However, drawing rights would not be restricted to the 18 to 27 year range, but could be utilized at any point in an individual's lifetime. In a major departure from the Tobin-Ross proposal, the full amount would be either taken or declined, i.e. prior to age 25 the individual would have to declare his intention to participate, at which point the full amount would become available (although not necessarily eligible for immediate withdrawal).

Having declared the intention to participate, a tax equal to a fixed percentage of total income, e.g., 6%, would be imposed in each year for a period of thirty years, beginning with age 18 (with the tax applied retroactively in case of a later declaration). Thus, surtax payments would cease at age 48. However, if at any prior point accumulated payments were sufficient to discharge a debt equal to 120% of the original total amount advanced, no further payment would be required. The individual would earn interest on the unexpended portion of the advance at the same rate at which interest would accrue on the outstanding debt (presumably equal to the rate then prevailing on federal debt). In any year, if income were zero, no payment would be made, and any positive payment could be made via a transfer from the unexpended endowment.

Drawings from the endowment account prior to age 48 would be limited to broadly defined human capital forming purposes, with limiting amounts determined by the level of direct educational costs (tuition and related fees) plus an annual living allowance. The only exceptions would be drawings utilized to make payments required on the basis of income. After age 48 any remaining endowment balance could be drawn upon for any purpose and in any amount. Effectively, after this age the endowment becomes a totally unrestricted asset of the individual.

3 Gösta Rehn, director of Manpower and Social Affairs at OECD in Paris has made a more far-reaching proposal of "one integrated system for financing all periods of non-work and providing a high degree of interchangeability, to be established instead of the present systems for youth education, adult studies, vacations, and retirement" (1972, p. 2). He argues that work, study, and leisure are all part of an adult continuum, and that individuals should be able to make more independent rational choices as to the pattern of work and life. He notes that industrial progress has enabled man to shorten progressively the length of the work week, but that irrational decisions are often made because individuals and society, collectively, have not had an opportunity to weigh and choose among alternatives. Assuming that continued economic progress permits a further reduction in the work week of one-fifth over the next decade or two, he raises the question as to whether there may be more attractive alternatives for society. For example, over a lifetime, a one-fifth reduction in the work week (if certain offsetting

factors are taken into account) is the equivalent of the alternative choice of adding three years to lifetime schooling, adding two weeks to annual vacations, lowering the retirement age by three years, and still reducing the work week by three hours. Yet piecemeal decisions (by law or labor contract) often preclude a systemic choosing between available alternatives.

Rehn, in a provocative paper for an OECD Conference on New Patterns for Working Time in 1972, proposed two "alternative futures." For the more ambitious integrated plan he presents the following possibility:

The financing of pensions, vacations, and off-the-job studies is consolidated into one integrated system to which payments are made by the employers on behalf of their workers along with all other social insurance fees as a percentage of wages. Self-employed persons also pay a similar proportion of their income according to tax assessments. The fees are calculated so as to cover the need for income maintenance during non-work periods. The compulsory belonging to this financing system gives everyone access to *drawing rights* which are so construed that their nonutilisation for the basically intended purpose gives — after a certain time — a right to use the same money for another purpose.[4]

The drawing rights include an advance credit which can be drawn upon before any fees have been paid so as to cover the costs of three years of studies immediately after compulsory school, (which has not been appreciably prolonged from now). Actual income-earning work and fee-paying gives the right to draw additional income maintenance to cover the expenditure for studies or other adjustments at any time in one's working life up to a limit of three year's study. Additional periods of study, before or after such additional drawing rights have been acquired, can be financed by an insured loan. The initial and accumulated study credits are growing with time so as to encourage and facilitate postponement of studies to periods when the annual income need is higher than during adolescence. In any competition for places in higher education, work experience is

---

[4] Part of the fees would in fact be a renaming of a certain part of presently paid taxes, covering the costs of secondary and higher education systems which can be used much more by some persons than by others. The individualised bookkeeping would also permit the latter one to draw appropriate advantages for purposes of their own choosing at any time in their lives. This "personalised income insurance and drawing rights system" (which incidentally is badly needed as a rationalisation of present notion conglomerate of income transfer arrangements) could also be combined with incentives inviting people to take time off during periods of economic slack in their own branch or area and thus to promote balance-keeping in the labour market. (Footnote and editorial amendments supplied by the author to provide greater conformity to latter edition.)

counted as positive points along with theoretical education achievements in secondary schools. No pressure is exerted on youths to continue school without interruption; on the contrary, vocational counselling advises them of the possibility of postponing studies (theoretical and practical) until they are more experienced and have more understanding of their own capabilities and interests, and of the situation and outlook in the labour market.

Of the annual vacation, three weeks must be taken each year, but the remaining three weeks can be accumulated and taken in longer sabbatical periods; those who wish to take their six weeks each year are encouraged to stagger them outside the peak season.

The concept of "ordinary retirement age" is largely abolished. Instead, individuals are continuously informed about the state of their accumulated rights and asked to choose their own combination of pension level and retirement age (or "temporary retirement") in the frame of possibilites created by their assets in the system. Provided his social insurance account has accumulated enough assets to cover a necessary minimum for the years after the age of say 62, (e.g., 30–40 per cent below what he would normally receive but never below a subsistence level) the individual can draw on his account to receive an early pension at periods of his own choosing, but return to earning a work income and to accumulating additional assets at any later time as well. For a person who has used his drawing rights for studies and sabbaticals to the full, however, the necessary minimum of assets on his account will not be reached until a relatively advanced age, perhaps some 50 years. (Early retirement because of disablement must of course be handled under special rules, just as presently.)

Maximum regular hours per week are 40 (or any present figure), but workers have an absolute right to go down to 35 (seven hours per day). This margin for controlled flexibility is used by some groups (trade unions, works councils) to negotiate regular prolongations (instead of unregulated but permanent overtime). Big-city groups with long daily travel and other inconveniences have utilized the right to go down to the lowest level, while groups of the opposite type have agreed to work a permitted maximum of 40 hours. The freedom to negotiate deviating hours of work is also used to provide for seasonal variations. Local agreements about various sorts of special allocation of hours and days for work, including individual "work à la carte" and part-time jobs, are widely used.

4   A fourth alternative possibility is adapting Rehn's concept to the American scene (Cartter, 1973). It foresees each young person at age 18 receiving a social security number and becoming eligible to draw on a personal social insurance account after a minimum period of employment in the work force. As indicated in a preceding section, every person upon reaching age 18 would have a four-year drawing right for up to half of tuition costs. Adult education would

be assisted by a supplemental system of contributions and benefits
—4 percent surcharge on earned income, perhaps half paid by em
ployer and half by employee, as in the case of social security, with
benefits as follows:

(1) After five years of employment each person would be eligible
to draw tax-exempt monthly subsistence payments equal to one
half of his average earnings in the preceding five years, with eligi
bility of one month for each year employed. For less than full-time
study, subsistence allowances would be prorated. (A maximum
allowance of, say, $1,000 per month might appropriately be set.

(2) Up to age 40, subsistence allowances would be available only
for participation in an approved educational or training program
Approval, however, would be extended relatively liberally to pro
prietary schools, programs conducted by trade unions and civic
associations, apprenticeship programs, and for vocational, pro
fessional, and general education.

(3) After age 40, eligibility credits could also be used for non
educational purposes, but only by using two months of accumulated
credit for each month of subsistence allotment drawn.

(4) Wives (or husbands) with no previous work experience would
be eligible to draw on their spouse's account at 50 percent benefi
levels.

(5) Any time after age 60, the unexpended balance in one's ac
count could either be exhausted as a terminal employment leave
benefit, or added to one's Old Age and Survivors Insurance (OASI
balance and reflected in higher pension benefits.

It is further proposed in this plan that, as expenditure offsets
unemployment compensation policy be modified so that benefits
would cover the first eight weeks of unemployment, and then be
reinstated only after accumulated educational leave eligibility had
been exhausted. A similar adjustment might be possible in the
case of public assistance for employable adults, and probably half
or more of federal expenditures on manpower training programs
could be eliminated. Instead of GI Bill education and training
benefits, the proposal suggests that, in the future, double credit
be granted for contributions for military or other special public
service employment. These savings would amount to approximately
$8 billion annually at the present rate of federal expenditure. Such

savings might be used to subsidize the income maintenance program for the first five years until it became self-financing, and could be used in the future for supplemental educational support.

Rehn has suggested that such plans might also be adapted to become a part of a positive manpower policy on the part of the federal government. Thus, in periods of unemployment and recession federal funds might be used to top-up benefits, thus encouraging a temporary expansion of the numbers availing themselves of educational opportunities.

These alternative proposals recognize that education ideally is a continuing, or recurrent, need, and they provide encouragement to individuals to make education a lifetime endeavor. Such plans would also remove much of the pressure on the young adult to complete education without interruption by assuring that financial assistance to meet both tuition and living costs would be available later in life. In addition, the individual who did not draw on his account for educational purposes would eventually receive a compensating benefit, unlike the case of the ordinary taxpayer today who contributes substantially to the cost of higher education whether or not he benefits directly from it.

Further, because it would be a contributory plan, controls over the kinds of institutions and types of educational programs pursued could be relatively relaxed. For the most part, taxpayers would be spending their own money, and should therefore be allowed considerable latitude of choice. (Protection against fraud or misleading claims, and perhaps undue profitability in schools, could be expected to remain a governmental responsibility as it is today under the GI Bill.) Under a contributory scheme the question of whether continuing education was vocational or avocational would be a matter of little consequence. Fine distinctions as to whether education was a form of investment or consumption would be immaterial. With tax contributions proportional to earned incomes, much or little income redistribution could be built into the plan by the nature and level of the established benefit ceiling.

Dresch has argued that "recurrent education represents a fracturing of the lockstep imposed by the traditional educational structure." Certainly, if increasing numbers of mature adults return to the classroom, there will have to be significant changes in our educational structure. Not only will adults be better motivated and more vocal in expressing their needs, but they will frequently require a different packaging of education than the somewhat leisurely pace at which it is now pursued on the assumption of full-time study for two or four years. Older students are more likely to know their own needs and be less degree-oriented in their desire to maximize brief recurring periods of further study. The critical question may be whether our traditional colleges and universities are prepared to receive this new class of students, or whether new institutions or new programs will have to emerge to serve them.

There seems little doubt, given the nature of today's society, that recurrent education is an increasingly important need; whether this need is converted into a "demand"—in the economist's sense of the word—hinges largely upon when and how society tackles the problem of financing. Adults are unlikely to be served well by merely adding on to the present arrangements for financing postsecondary education; rather, it seems evident that a bold new program of universal lifetime financing will be required. Several Western and Eastern European nations are considerably ahead of the United States in these developments. We may have to take a giant stride ahead if we are to maintain our greatest source of comparative economic advantage—the presence of a vast reservoir of highly educated manpower.

5. General Objectives

In the preceding sections of this report we have presented some of the issues involved in adjusting our institutions of postsecondary education to historical developments that place them in new circumstances. We have indicated a need for some of our college and universities to accommodate new types of learners—particularly returning dropouts and stopouts and adults. We have raised some of the issues involved in funding life-long educational opportunities for all Americans. And, finally, we have suggested that one's view of postsecondary education in the United States must be wide-angled, including not only the familiar centers of higher education, but also the full range of schools, institutions and programs that constitute a richly diverse but underutilized resource for education beyond high school.

In encouraging a view that places colleges and universities within the totality of postsecondary education, we do not believe that all institutions of postsecondary education are alike, that the differences between them are to be ignored, or that efforts should be made to eliminate or obscure the most distinctive characteristics of the different educational channels to life and work. American postsecondary education is not a blend, but rather an array of diverse institutions and programs. There should be freer use of institutions from the full width of the spectrum by students of all ages, but the education thus obtained should not necessarily be interchangeable from one type of institution to another.

Throughout our discussion of general objectives that follows we assume that there is an important distinction between learning experience and educational experience. Learning experience can take a variety of formal and informal forms. To a considerable extent, it is acquired just by living. But most individual learning experiences are isolated, unplanned, and unintegrated into any pre-

determined conceptual framework. The educational experience, or
the other hand, is a coherent one, often requiring that the things
that are taught are coordinated with the method and environment
of the instruction.

Students who keep these distinctions in mind should be able to
utilize the rich postsecondary educational resources of this country
with more precision. Those who seek knowledge about a specific
subject but do not wish to commit themselves to a full-blown college
program will be able to do so. Those who wish to supplement col-
lege-based learning with skill development can do so with a clearer
notion of the difference between the two activities.

If our policy-makers in education keep these distinctions in mind,
they will come to regard many of the learning experiences that are
currently available outside colleges and universities as vital exten-
sions of the resources of this country for education — for certain subjects are learned as well in private specialized schools, for example,
as they are in colleges.

But this enlarged view of postsecondary education raises some
questions of a broad nature that need resolution. The solutions
may be very difficult and even impossible until we have settled
other pending problems in postsecondary education. For example,
the question of providing funding for students who elect to study
in institutions other than colleges and universities may have to
await definitive action on funding proposals for higher education
now pending as matters of public policy.

We see problems of this type arising in the funding of postsecondary education, the provision of adequate educational opportunities, the coordination of postsecondary education, the accreditation of systems of higher education, the recognition of student achievement in postsecondary education, and the development
of counseling and information centers for nontraditional students.

**FUNDING
LIFE-LONG
LEARNING**
In our report *Less Time, More Options* we recommended:

. . . that all persons, after high school graduation, have two years of postsecondary education placed "in the bank" for them, to be withdrawn at
any time of their lives when it best suits them (Carnegie Commission,
1971a, p. 20).

In this report we reconfirm that recommendation and submit
more detailed suggestions on how that proposal might be put into
effect.

General Objective 1: Every person will have available to him, throughout his life, financial assistance for at least two years of postsecondary education. For at least part of the entitlement, there will be no restrictions as to the type of educational institution the recipient might elect to attend.

PROVISION OF EDUCATIONAL OPPORTU- NITIES

Our Commission has repeatedly asserted that state governments should exercise the major responsibility for providing postsecondary education in the United States. Recognition that postsecondary education includes not only colleges and universities, but also many other institutions and programs, enlarges that responsibility. Our states need to continue to provide and support academic institutions; in addition, and without diminishing such support, they must assure that, within the full range of educational resources made available under both public and private auspices, there are sufficient places to serve the widely divergent needs of all their potential learners.

General Objective 2: The states will make adequate provision, within the full spectrum of their postsecondary education resources, for educational opportunities adequate to the divergent needs of all their citizens.

PLANNING AND COORDINA- TION

A single, integrated system of postsecondary education with well-defined, generally accepted educational goals would probably not require an external planning agency. Decisions relating to parts of the system would be funneled through a single administrative decision-making authority. In such a system there would be considerable uniformity of operational styles, regulatory standards, financing techniques, and governance patterns. But it is doubtful that such a system could encompass the multiplicity of goals, the range of governance and operational patterns, and responsiveness to different constituencies found in all sectors of American postsecondary education, without either restraining variations of missions or programs or becoming massive in its organizational structure. In the totality of postsecondary education, the present diversity of purposes, techniques, operations, and funding patterns must be preserved, and the best approach is to leave the individual sectors within the system as autonomous as possible. But broad planning and information gathering and study are also essential. We recognized this need in our report *The Capitol and the Campus* and recommended that state planning agencies charged with responsibility for postsecondary education:

. . . take into account the present and potential contributions to state needs of all types of postsecondary institutions including universities, colleges, private trade and technical schools, area vocational schools, industry, unions, and other agencies providing various forms of postsecondary education.

The interests of such agencies should also:

. . . encompass the entire time span of a person's postsecondary education needs from immediately after high school throughout life.

While such broadly scoped planning is essential in a system which has a plurality of objectives and institutions and agencies, it is equally essential that the type of planning required not be viewed as that which takes on regulatory or administrative functions. Beneficial efforts of information sharing and coordinate activities that foster optimal institutional interaction and development of distinct educational purposes for various organizations can be quickly turned into disadvantages if the agency which acquires those powers and functions moves toward conformity and standardization or utilizes its influence to subvert state responsibility for the adequate support of higher education.

General Objective 3: State coordinating agencies will become increasingly aware of the resources of all postsecondary educational institutions in their states and, in partnership with those affected, will utilize their influence to assure adequate financial support for their institutions and to minimize unnecessary duplication of specialized programs in colleges and universities and other institutions offering postsecondary education.

INFORMATION AND COUNSELING The most important step that can be taken to improve the usefulness of the full range of postsecondary education activities in the United States is the development of more adequate information about them. In this regard, colleges and universities are the very visible parts of an iceberg. Counselors and prospective students have access to many sources of information about them. This is not the case for other institutions and programs for postsecondary education.

A few efforts are now being made to develop such information. Of particular importance are the recent and ongoing efforts of the Office of Education to survey adult participation in postsecondary education and to compile an inventory of vocational schools. But much remains to be done.

In gathering information, the following principle should be considered:

- Meaningful information on noncollegiate postsecondary education cannot be collected by simply obtaining data from this universe using terminology developed for data on colleges and universities.

- While coordination of data-collection projects should be centralized for the purpose of maintaining consistent definitions and compatible units, there are advantages to decentralizing data collection, either on a regional or state basis or on the basis of subsets of postsecondary institutions and activities.

- The type of data to be collected should be determined on the basis of public policy need and potential learner need.

Once data is collected, it should be widely available. One useful form of dissemination is the information catalog. The *New York Times Guide to Continuing Education in America* is a successful prototype of such a publication, although many students and counselors might find directories that are regional in scope to be of value as well.

General Objective 4: Collection and dissemination of information on all forms of postsecondary education will be given high priority by federal and state educational statistical agencies.

General Objective 5: Education Opportunity Counseling Centers, such as those recommended in our report *The Campus and the City* (Carnegie Commission, 1972a), and other appropriate local agencies will have as one of their responsibilities the development and distribution of information about postsecondary educational resources including, but also in addition to, colleges and universities.

CERTIFICATION OF ACHIEVEMENT AND PERFORMANCE

Postsecondary education today is characterized by many purposes, a variety of forms and modes of operation, and a genuine plurality of control. All of these differences are useful in a learning society. Not everyone needs or wants the same kind of education.

Difficulties are encountered, however, when an attempt is made to translate certification of learning in one setting into certification of learning in another setting.

Certification occurs at four main points in postsecondary education:

The *first* occurs when a student is admitted to an institution of learning. At this point an evaluation is made of the student's ability, usually measured by past achievement, to undertake and complete studies at a given college. The certification is by the institution admitting the student and is made according to that institution's own standards. Admission to a highly selective institution may inferentially demonstrate a student's ability to study at any college or university, but it specifically demonstrates ability only to study at the institution to which the student is admitted.

The *second* certification involves the quality of the institution itself. It now takes the form of accreditation, usually by an association of similar institutions. It may also take the form of validation by government. The fact of accreditation means that an institution meets standards set by its peers. Validation means that an institution meets minimum conditions essential to the public interest.

The *third* certification involves the awarding of credits and degrees for student achievement. This requires an evaluation of the individual, and the standards employed are again those of the institution. A degree from one institution does not really mean that a student has achieved the same competencies that students with the same degree from other institutions have. Institutions vary in their requirements for degrees. There are sometimes even variations in requirements among divisions within a single institution. Moreover, some institutions give students considerable latitude in deciding for themselves which combination of courses and experiences will be recognized with certification or a degree, while others do not.

The *fourth* certification involves the acceptance of a person as competent for certain types of employment. Recognition of achievements by a college or university—through a degree—may be a factor in such certification, but the certification itself is a function of those who set the standards for the occupations or professions to be entered. These may be employers—or in the cases of licensed occupations and professions—state agencies or professional associations.

The most important evaluation, in many respects, is the accreditation of institutions. Accreditation may entitle institutions to certain kinds of government subsidy, or to the privilege under state law to offer certain kinds of education. It also legitimates the degrees and credits institutions give to their graduates and students—and thus facilitates the transfer of such recognition to other institutions.

Three different types of criteria could conceivably be used for accrediting institutions.

The first criterion considers the "inputs" made to achieve quality—the number and competency of the faculty, the average ability of the students, the availability and quality of facilities for instruction, and the breadth or depth of course offering. These criteria apply to the resources of an institution, and they are moot on whether or not the resources are used appropriately or well. Because many of the input factors are quantifiable, and because colleges and universities have had long experience with evaluations based on them, they are widely regarded as both objective and sound.

The second criterion involves processes—the nature and sequence of what happens at an institution. To date, we have virtually no useful experience with this kind of evaluation, and it is doubtful that adequate measures could be developed for making it effective.

The third criterion involves "outputs"—the consequences of attending a given institution. Some postsecondary institutions, such as trade and technical schools, have attempted to measure output in terms of numbers of students placed in jobs, student satisfaction as determined by follow-up surveys, and the like. Other institutions are paying increasing attention to the identification of specific objectives that should be realized by students who have completed learning tasks designed into the instruction that is offered.

We realize that there is much investigating and experimenting to be done before output measures for purposes of accreditation enjoy the confidence that input measures do now. There is also some danger that institutions may prematurely grasp upon irrelevant, trivial, or untested output measures in evaluating their own quality and performance. But we nevertheless advocate a cautious but continued effort to develop and improve output measures with reference to particular institutional goals as standards for accreditation and regulation and decreasing reliance upon standardized input measures alone. Our reasons are:

1 Excellent and abundant inputs can be ill-managed or inappropriately allocated to such an extent that they do not perform the functions for which they are intended.

2 Emphasis on inputs for evaluation of institutions encourages colleges to seek resources to finance facilities and programs which may be standard for certain other (usually prestigious) institutions — but may not be essential for their own missions.

3 Input measures tend to apply to total institutions rather than to individual programs. A weak department at a prestigious institution may be accorded more recognition off the campus than an even stronger department at a generally weaker institution.

4 By utilizing input measures, it is easier for graduates seeking employment to trade upon the prestige of their school rather than upon their own individual competencies.

5 Output measures apply to what an institution does in accordance with its announced mission and not just to what an institution has at its disposal.

6 Input measures tend to keep unconventional institutions out of the mainstream of educational endeavor, even when the results of their efforts are demonstrably good.

Institutions of postsecondary education, testing organizations, and agencies of the federal government concerned with education should continue efforts to develop reliable output measures for evaluating institutions of learning. Until such measures are available, however, we must continue to apply input measures as impartially as we can.

As government support for both institutions and students increases, the general public has a growing stake in the effectiveness of the accreditation system. Citizens will not want their governments to support study at institutions of little or no worth. At the same time, they may want their government to support study at some institutions that offer specific kinds of training in an effective way at costs lower than those encountered at institutions accredited by associations.

Accommodating these legitimate public interests could pose serious problems in autonomy for postsecondary education. To forestall those problems, we must eventually adopt two systems for certifying institutions. One would be a private system, similar to the one that is currently operative, that attests to the detailed effectiveness of institutions as compared to other institutions of the same type. The second system would be administered by the government and would validate minimal standards of institutional stability and integrity. This system will be increasingly important not only to guide investment of public funds in postsecondary education, but also to protect the prospective student. Among the significant measures for validation will be fiscal soundness, legitimacy of advertising claims, quality of faculty as determined by their training and/or experience, and, to the extent the information is available, the usefulness of the instruction given as evaluated by representative former students.

General Objective 6: The current system of accreditation by institutional associations will be supplemented by a second system instituted by state and federal governments for the purpose of validating fiscal stability, legitimacy of advertising claims, and general quality of instruction. Those responsible for administering such validation will be restrained, by all means feasible, from regulation of postsecondary education and will seek to establish minimum rather than optimum standards for the accreditation they are empowered to bestow.

CREDITING STUDENT ACHIEVEMENT With the growing awareness that education in nonacademic institutions can be valuable both to an individual and to society, suggestions have been made that the traditional definition of the B.A. degree be broadened to include components of experience, vocational education, and training.

It is at this juncture that our Commission would offer a reminder that the traditional college degree originally meant more than mastery of a specific body of knowledge or the endurance of a student through some specified period of study and lectures. It meant (and at many institutions still means) completion of an education that was deliberately planned to meet certain objectives set by the institutions awarding the degree. A degree from Brown University, for instance, indicated not only completion of a certain number of courses, but completion of courses planned by the faculty as a coherent unit and offered in a particular environment created and sustained by Brown University.

Inroads on this view have been made by the recent redefinition of degrees on some campuses in terms of a specific number of degree credits, with the subject-content and combinations of courses left to the option of individual students.

Further inroads have been made by according new importance to education obtained outside academic institutions. In some instances, life experience, often unevaluated in terms of the competence it has produced or the academic goals it has served, is recognized for degree credit.

There may be some value in substituting life experience for certain prerequisites required for the pursuit of advanced learning. For example, experience leading to acceptable competence as a draftsman might be substituted for a drafting course required for engineers or architects. But the substitution need not carry degree credit. Its advantage should be that of expediting the progress of study, and not of collecting points toward a degree.

Traditional degrees have high status, and whenever degree credit is given for some type of nonacademic activity, it tends to invest that activity with some of the recognition accorded to the degree itself. The extension of this practice is inherently disadvantageous because:

- The B.A. degree loses its value as an indicator of a particular level and type of educational accomplishment.

- Translating all postsecondary educational experiences into a common unit obscures real differences that, in the interest of diversity, intelligent public policy, and individual educational planning, should be maintained.

- The practice could gradually transform colleges from educational institutions into credentialing, legitimizing institutions for all types of postsecondary educational activities.

The time has come for establishment of a more rational and more communicative system of showing accomplishment of educational goals than is possible through the present degree system. One feature of that system should be the development of ways to recognize student achievement at more frequent intervals. We have elsewhere suggested the availability of degrees in two-year modules.

General Objective 7: Colleges and universities will successfully resist pressures to grant degree credit for those activities and experiences that are not clearly planned as part of an academic learning program designed to meet the educational goals recognized by the degrees offered.

General Objective 8: Institutions of postsecondary education will grant degrees, certificates, and honors at more frequent intervals than they now do.

General Objective 9: Undergraduate and professional degrees will increasingly become only a part of the cumulative record of an individual's educational accomplishments. Ultimately, the degrees will become less important than the total record as evidence of such accomplishments.

We believe that such a system will make possible the identification of each individual's educational accomplishments by specifying particular educational goals, educational activities undertaken, and levels of accomplishment for such goals.

The United States prides itself on the diversity of its postsecondary education. And much evidence of that diversity is currently available, particularly as one moves from the narrower universe of higher education to the broader universe of postsecondary education. But there is also some growing and disturbing evidence that some of the valuable distinctions may disappear as all institutions attempt to feed into the degree process. The true recognition of an individual's many-faceted educational accomplishments should neither be obscured by a general-purpose degree nor should all postsecondary institutions and the activities leading to those accomplishments be forced to conform to standards and artificial units of measure once found appropriate for narrowly defined academic accomplishments.

6. *Specific Objectives*

In this section we narrow the discussion to suggest specific objectives that might be sought in our endeavors to move more surely toward a learning society. Some of the objectives concern particular types of education and specific alternatives to colleges and universities as sources of learning. Others involve fairly specific issues that arise from an expanded view of postsecondary education. Whereas most of the general objectives discussed in the previous section of this report and long range, the specific objectives discussed in this section tend to be short range. Many of them, in fact, could be achieved by immediate action.

ADULT AND PART-TIME STUDENTS IN COLLEGES AND UNIVERSITIES

Much has already been done to extend educational opportunities beyond high school to young persons previously denied them because of inadequate financial resources, discrimination, or the lack of institutions prepared to admit them and help them overcome deficiencies in educational preparation. But this progress has most strongly benefited persons in the 17- to 21-year age group who undertake full-time studies.

Many older people in our society were simply born too soon to take advantage of the kinds of assistance and facilities that are now available to our nation's youth. And demand for education among adults is growing. The sheer size of the pool of "adults" in the most educationally active age group 20 to 29 continues to increase—from 30.9 million in 1970 to an anticipated 40.5 million by 1980 (U.S. Bureau of the Census, 1971, pp. 13–14). The education level of adults is also increasing, and, as indicated elsewhere in this report, there is a strong correlation between participation in adult learning activity and educational attainment. Moreover, there are many trends in American society that will stimulate more demand for lifelong learning.

As the stock of human knowledge increases, there will be mor for the learning man to know. As scientific research continues, nev knowledge will lead to the improvement of our technology and wil increase our productivity; life will become more complex and harde to understand without the acquisition of still more knowledge. A specialization increases, certain occupations will disappear; som will be redesigned; new ones will emerge. Increasing meritocrac will require maximum cultivation of an individual's talents an abilities. To exercise more influence and to participate in mor activities outside the home, women will want opportunities to lear new skills, occupational abilities, and professions.

These same pressures will push many young persons who hav dropped out of postsecondary institutions back toward learnin activities. And many of these prospective learners are also disad vantaged in their desire to return to college. They, too, lack acces to support funds, and often need to mesh studies and full-tim work. Some of them need or desire educational opportunities in dif ferent environments from those that are offered in conventiona college programs.

Colleges and universities have provided education for adul students for a long time. But it is often offered in a spirit of publi service or public relations (Penfield, 1972) and is not always of th same quality as the education colleges offer to regular students.

BARRIERS TO THE NEW LEARNERS If colleges and universities are to provide education for the new learners, they must either remove certain barriers that currentl exist, or provide alternative ways for such persons to participat in their educational programs.

Procedural barriers Because many of the requirements imposed upon students of colleges and universities were designed for young persons who have just completed high school, they, perhaps inad vertently, become barriers to older students.

Admissions requirements characteristically involve examination of high school records to determine whether certain subject and grade prerequisites have been met. Such requirements reflect cur rent high school grading practices and may not be applicable to the transcripts of older students.

Much of the testing and advising associated with admission to colleges is conducted through or in cooperation with high school counselors. For that reason, information about testing and college admissions procedures may not be readily available to older persons nor to persons neither currently or recently enrolled in high schools.

Course loads are normally designed for full-time students who are presumed to have predictable amounts of time at their disposal for classroom attendance and independent study.

If full-time minimum course loads are required for all students, the work may be too time consuming for persons who must hold a full-time job or meet family responsibilities while they are pursuing educational objectives.

Finally, schedules of instruction may be such that all courses requisite to completion of a learning program desired by a part-time student are offered only during his working hours.

Environmental barriers Compulsory attendance at student body meetings or chapel; early closing of libraries; inordinate numbers of class cancellations for athletic events; unreasonable regulations of personal conduct on campus (such as early curfews); attempts to impose collegiate traditions (for example, requiring freshmen to wear distinctive items of clothing); and avoidable "herding" of students into time-consuming lines might have to be relaxed if large numbers of adult or part-time students are to be accommodated on some campuses. We do not recommend that institutions abandon all traditions that have meaning for them, but we do suggest that some traditions and regulations may have to be traded away if new learners are to find a campus attractive.

Psychological barriers Among some older persons and some college and university instructors, the belief that one's ability to learn diminishes with age sometimes stands in the way of education. Scientific studies of learning ability indicate that there is nothing inherent in the aging process itself that impairs mental ability.[1] Individuals with different life experiences may have different mental abilities—but this variation does not correlate entirely with age. To the degree that the older adult's capacities to participate in higher educational activity are affected by slower speed and weakened sensory acuities, it seems unlikely that they differ greatly from some of the younger students—including some with more severe handicaps—who are already accepted on our campuses without

[1] See, for example, Lorge (1955) and Owens and Charles (1963).

prejudices. Adults may be more interested in knowledge that they can apply to life and work situations, and less interested in theoretical knowledge. If they have been unaccustomed to studying and taking tests for a long period of time, it may require special effort on their part to refresh those skills to a point where they can be competitive with younger schoolmates who have concentrated on such activities more continuously. Differences such as these do deserve recognition. They may call for special attention from instructors, but they should not make older students feel incapable of learning, or make instructors feel that older students cannot learn.

Financial barriers Student assistance programs of state and national government, and of most institutions of higher learning are developed almost entirely for the benefit of full-time, younger students. Many younger students also receive help from their parents. Most prospective learners who wish to enter postsecondary learning programs on a part-time basis must do so at night, must have the cooperation of their employers,[2] or must forfeit salaries or wages lost during time spent in class. In addition, they must pay the fees charged for their instruction. Women with children must also pay for child care. As we pointed out in Section 4, little assistance is available to any of these part-time learners.

Institutional barriers Institutions can lose money by admitting part-time students unless the instruction given to such students is offered entirely as a part of the regular curriculum. They may have difficulty in getting able faculty members to teach at night or at other times that may be most convenient for part-time students. Moreover, some faculty members are inclined to downgrade the importance of such instruction and consider part-time students less capable than full-time students.

These barriers can be overcome. Some procedural barriers, particularly those involving instruction, are beginning to come down as institutions introduce policies that make learning more convenient, attractive, and effective for all of their students.

---

[2] Some firms refund tuition expenses to encourage their employees to engage in part-time education. Others occasionally grant workers time-off, or adjusted work schedules to accommodate educational activity.

OPTIONS FOR INSTITUTIONS Confronted with new demands for educational opportunity by adult and part-time students, we believe that colleges and universities should be free to choose whether to adjust their instructional programs to accommodate them or not. Some institutions may prefer to provide educational experiences only for younger students in a completely youth-oriented environment. A fully diversified system of higher education should certainly be able to include such institutions without difficulty. Other colleges and universities that now offer instruction mainly or entirely for younger full-time students may find their physical resources underutilized because of declining enrollments. They should be encouraged to consider adopting programs that would attract the new adult and part-time learners.

For most institutions, there are three methods of accommodating the new learners:

- By integrating part-time instruction with the instruction offered by the regular departments of colleges and universities
- By creating special evening or extension divisions to accommodate these students
- By creating separate institutions or organizations to provide part-time continuing and recurrent education at the postsecondary level

We believe that, to the extent possible, colleges and universities should incorporate degree-credit instruction for all students, full-time and part-time, into their regular departmental offerings. Although some observers have noted resistance of young students to programs in which they join in classes with older people, there are also instances, for example, in special courses offered at the University of Utah, where students are enthusiastic about such opportunities. By providing more opportunities for part-time students to participate in regular instruction, colleges and universities will serve not only many adults, but also many younger students who must support themselves with employment while they pursue their education.

We also believe that as older students become more evident on our campuses, and as more instruction is offered with their time limitations in mind, the need to offer degree-credit instruction to adults through separate administrative or academic divisions diminishes. Where degree-credit instruction is provided equally to full- and part-time students, we believe that the temptation of institutions to utilize their facilities for offering instruction to adults or part-time students that is not at a level, or of a kind, appropriate to the academic character of the institution is mitigated. Community colleges, which must be responsive to the demands of local constituents, are particularly susceptible to demands for such instruction and, as long as the desired instruction does not exceed their academic capacities, they probably should continue their tradition of providing it. But while most colleges may provide cultural opportunities to their communities in the form of concerts, lectures, and other such events, they would be prudent to resist temptations to offer nondegree, or recreational instruction of a prolonged, systematic character on their own campuses. They would serve learning better by joining with neighboring institutions in the formation of organizations in which such instruction could be offered under completely independent management although existing campus facilities might be utilized.

Separate divisions *within* an institution are not suitable solutions to the problem of providing part-time instruction for the future's new learners. Such divisions are often weak, starved financially by their parent institutions, and ignored or disdained by faculty members of the regular academic departments. In their efforts to sustain themselves through fees, separate divisions find it difficult to resist offering instruction that is out of keeping with the character of the academic objectives and standards of the parent institution, but which is popular with their clients.

We particularly emphasize the importance of offering instruction only at levels where an institution has competence. Two-year colleges should not offer part-time, adult, or continuing education at the upper-division level of four-year colleges and universities. Comprehensive four-year institutions should not offer part-time or continuing instruction at the postbaccalaureate level except in subjects in which they are authorized and accredited to offer such instruction as part of their regular programs. When institutions that are geographically isolated from higher-level colleges or universities discern a local need for instruction beyond their competency, they can preserve the integrity of both their own and other institutions' educational offerings if they suggest that an institution that has such competency offer the needed instruction through special cooperative arrangements. If such demands for instruction persist and are numerous, a separate, cooperative organization with access to institutions with a wide range of competencies might be formed to devise and administer the needed programs.

Some colleges and universities charge part-time students fees for instruction that are set not only to cover instructional costs to the institutions, but also to render a margin of income that can be applied to other institutional expenses. Within a single institution, we do not believe that part-time students should pay more for the same instruction given to full-time students than the full-time students do. Institutions, however, are justified in charging part-time students the full costs of instruction that is offered mainly as recreation or entertainment. Colleges are also justified in charging the full cost of advanced education offered to employed specialists or professionals who are seeking occupational or professional upgrading through special educational programs. With only these exceptions, fees should be equitable for full-time and part-time students.

With respect to instruction for adult and part-time students in colleges and universities, we believe that efforts should be made to realize the following specific objectives:

Specific Objective 1: The provision of part-time learning opportunities will be considered a legitimate function of all colleges or universities, regardless of their level of instruction or type of control. After deliberation, some institutions will elect not to perform this function, but their decisions will be based on particular objectives they have set for themselves because of educational policy options, limitations of space, finances, or facilities, and not on a belief that such instruction is inherently inappropriate to colleges and universities.

Specific Objective 2: Once admitted to a college or university for academic studies, qualified part-time students will be eligible to take courses in the regular departments of the institution and will be accorded the same campus privileges that are accorded to full-time students.

Specific Objective 3: Wherever academic programs are offered for students who are adults of all ages, the rules for student conduct, campus traditions, and the learning environment will be hospitable to them, and will not discriminate against older students.

Specific Objective 4: Institutions of higher education will not offe
part-time students courses that exceed levels of instruction mair
tained in courses offered to full-time students. Two-year institu
tions will not offer upper-division or professional instruction t
part-time students. Vocational schools that do not offer genera
education to full-time students will not offer it to part-time student:

PRIVATE SPECIALTY SCHOOLS Private specialty schools comprise a large segment of postsecondar
education and are now the focal point of considerable new interesi
They are usually referred to as *proprietary schools* or as *privat
trade and technical schools.* But both terms are too narrow for ou
purposes. Many of the schools in this category continue to be oper
ated for profit but others are not. Nor are all of the schools in thi
category vocational schools. Many of them offer courses that ar
primarily directed toward leisure activities. For these reasons w
have rejected the more common terms and are referring to th
schools in this report as *private specialty schools.* We include i
these schools those with the following characteristics.

- Have programs limited to one subject or a group of closely relate
subjects

- Operate as a private institution, with either profit or nonprofi
status for tax purposes

- Serve students who are either high school graduates or beyon
high school–leaving age (usually 18)

- Operate either as a day school, night school, or correspondenc
school, or any combination of these

- Do not generally offer college-level degrees

The Educational Policy Research Center at Syracuse University
estimated that there were 9.6 million students in such schools in
1970 (Moses, 1971, p. 19).

Including only those specialty schools that offer primarily voca
tional education, Belitsky (1969, p. 8) estimated that there wer
7,000 such schools in 1966 serving about 1.5 million students.

In 1971, almost 5,000 specialty vocational schools enrolled on
or more students receiving veteran's educational benefits. And, ir
1972, utilizing lists supplied by state education departments
occupational school directories, and telephone books, a Carnegi
Commission sponsored study identified some 2,600 private spe
cialty vocational schools in 11 large-population states.

The regulation and supervision of private specialty schools present a special problem. In many states, they are viewed as business operations and do not come under the jurisdiction of state education authorities, but, instead, under the business codes. As a result, their educational activities are subject to general governmental scrutiny only to the extent that a business licensing board has been established to control minimum licensing entries into the field. These minimum standards indirectly affect at least the minimum content and time distribution of subjects studied but may not relate directly to the quality of practices of the educational institution involved. This pattern is particularly prevalent, for example, in barbering, cosmetics, and health fields — fields concerned with services to the person.

Many states have enacted general responsibility statutes which require that the school operation provide evidence of good character (usually character references or affidavits of state residents) and fiscal responsibility (usually a bond or a history of responsible operation). More recently, such statutes have included provisions relating to advertising and soliciting standards. Where this has occurred, the "truth in advertising" standards applied to private specialty schools may well be more stringent than anything required of colleges and universities.

Private associations of special schools which include accrediting services among their activities also exist. For example, the National Association for Trade and Technical Schools, the United Business Schools Association, and the National Home Study Council provide this service as do also associations operating in the cosmetology and health fields. But the number of schools in operation in any of these fields is often far greater than the number that have sought the accrediting services of the association. This does not always say anything about the quality of the school, since certain schools choose not to pay the high fees or go through the effort of seeking accreditation and may not see any offsetting benefits — particularly if their enrollment and financial condition are satisfactory.

Three other forms of approval of certification with reference to these schools have emerged in recent years.

1 Schools wishing to be approved for students carrying veteran's educational benefits must satisfy certain requirements — usually related to their general responsibility and their fair treatment of students (such as tuition refund policy).

2 Approval for participation in state and federal student-aid pro grams.

3 A new trend in which a few states have authorized such schools to grant degrees.

While the first two forms of validation are usually quite general — attesting only to the nature of the school's activity and fiscal responsibility — the third type of approval has applied rigid quantitative standards to the school's operations. It is interesting that at a time when accreditation practices in colleges and universities are getting looser, those applied to schools gaining entrance to this field appear highly rigid — specifying in some instances the minimum classroom hours, the maximum student-faculty ratio, and the distribution of time between general and special education.

There must, however, be minimum controls to protect prospective students from fraudulent advertising and programs, and to protect the vast majority of legitimate and effective schools from being tarnished by the dishonesty or incompetence of a few schools.

Specific Objective 5: States will periodically review their statutes to make certain that they adequately protect students against fraudulent claims and unfair business practices that may characterize operations of some private specialty schools.

ELEMENTARY AND SECONDARY SCHOOLS In Table 5 of this report, we noted that about 3.9 million adults participated in education offered at elementary and secondary schools. They accounted for 5.3 percent of the program enrollments tabulated.

The activities of elementary and secondary schools are basically beyond the scope of the inquiries made by the Carnegie Commission on Higher Education although we have commented, from time to time, on matters in which these schools and the colleges and universities have a mutual interest. In this report, it seems appropriate to note that the adult and continuing education programs of elementary and secondary schools have been significant learning resources. In general, they offer instruction at levels appropriate to their facilities and competency, and they give to many Americans a "second chance" to acquire, in their own communities, basic skill and learning — for example, reading, writing, and arithmetic — they were unable to get in their youth, or to learn about general subjects they have not been able to pursue at other institutions.

Specific Objective 6: Elementary and secondary schools will continue to play a significant role in the provision of educational
opportunities appropriate to their resources to persons of all ages
in the communities where they are located.

BUSINESS AND INDUSTRY The educational endeavors of business and industry range from
providing on-the-job training to large-scale schools created to train
specialists to filling key positions in development and research
programs and company management.

In a 1967 study that sought to determine the extent of college-
level educational activities in industry, three general types of
education were identified: (1) the updating of scientists and engineers, (2) management training, and (3) introduction of new technology. The study reported that annual higher education expenditures in industry in 1967 amounted to "nearly 20 billion dollars,
spent by approximately 85 percent of the major industries in
America" (Torpey, 1967, p. 408). Thus, according to this study,
in 1967 industry spent more on scientific, management, and new
technology training programs within industry than was spent
through all of the private and public colleges in the nation for all
types of college level education.

In 1962, the U.S. Department of Labor conducted a study of
involvement of business and industrial firms in training activities.
Training programs were defined as any prearranged formal system
of instruction sponsored by the employer or by employer-union
agreement and designed to improve the ability of employees to perform their current or future job duties. It included instruction for
employees both on and off the job site. The major findings were:

1 Of the 711,000 establishments responding to the survey, one out
of every five sponsored some type of formal training.

2 Of the 37 million workers employed in the responding establishments, 2.7 million were actually enrolled in an employer-sponsored
training program.

3 The larger the establishment, the greater the probability that a
training program was in operation (U.S. Bureau of Labor Statistics,
1962).

This study by the Department of Labor may underestimate the importance of industrial educational activities. In other studies in

which informal on-the-job training is also included, it become
clear that the majority of workers, even in skilled crafts, acquir
their skills through the informal process of on-the-job trainin
rather than through formal classroom instruction (Somers & Roon
kin, 1972).

About 80 percent of the educational activities of business and ir
dustry are concerned with vocational education (Johnstone
Rivera, 1963, p. 65). But the range of subject matter include
general education, agriculture, hobbies, and recreation, home an
family, personal development, and public affairs. A substanti
number of employers are also involved in safety or orientatio
courses.

To the extent that industry and postsecondary institutions shar
common educational goals, it is likely that mutually benefici
linkages would develop between the two. Some have. Cooperativ
education, which combines work experience with a college-degre
program, various types of university and college-sponsored sho
courses for management personnel, and tuition reimbursemer
programs are some of the interactions that have developed. Cc
operative education, or "sandwich education" as it is referred t
in Great Britain (where it was introduced in Scotland in 1880 an
England in 1903), was first used in this country in 1905 at th
University of Cincinnati. In 1971, there were cooperative educatio
programs at 225 colleges and universities (Wilson, 1972, p. 3).

As explained by Ralph W. Tyler, such programs enable student
to practice skills and knowledge learned in school, gain a realisti
understanding of tasks involved in an occupation, explore alte
native occupational careers, and develop realistic work attitude
Students also get opportunities to "observe adults making dec
sions in various contexts; furthermore, and of particular signif
cance, they themselves have many opportunities to make decision
and to see their consequences" (Tyler, 1972, p. 21).

Not all education-industry linkages have been successful, how
ever. Companies often find that well-motivated employees withou
vocational training in a college learn specific job skills as well a
do employees who have had such training. Moreover, workers wh
have had only vocational education are frequently found to be un
able to adjust to technological changes. A report issued by th
National Association of Manufacturers (1970) indicates that
common complaint of vocational school education by industry i

that it often trains students for specific jobs that are no longer needed within a broad occupation.

To overcome some of the most important inadequacies of education-industry linkages, we should work toward the following specific objectives:

Specific Objective 7: College- and school-based vocational education will emphasize general knowledge common to broad groups of occupations in addition to providing training for specific skills. Industry will continue to accept responsibility for training persons to perform skills required by specific tasks on the job.

Specific Objective 8: When they do not have skill-training expertise in their own companies, businesses will seek agreements with educational institutions to provide technical aid for the development of industry-based skill-training programs and for the evaluation of such programs.

Specific Objective 9: Research and development funds will be made available by the Office of Education and the Department of Labor to facilitate the development of the theoretical knowledge and technical expertise needed to service agreements between post-secondary educational institutions and industry for the development of skill-training programs.

Specific Objective 10: Educational institutions that have well-developed instructional technology will avail businesses and industry of opportunities to tie plant-site classrooms to televised instruction originating on the campus, and will make available audio-videotape instruction or computer-assisted instruction on subjects relevant to business and industry training programs.

APPRENTICE-SHIP PROGRAMS Regardless of how much formal education people receive, they must learn most of the skills and procedures needed in their work after they are employed. Such instruction is usually provided by either one's supervisor or designated mentors, and the practice is found not only in skilled occupations but, in sophisticated forms, in the professions.

The formalization of this process through apprenticeships has a long and, on the whole, successful history and its expansion deserves consideration. In the United States, apprenticeships began to take their present form in the early twentieth century and both the Smith-Hughes Act of 1917 and the Fitzgerald Act of 193' gave impetus to their development. Official standards for apprenticeship programs under the Fitzgerald Act are:

(1) At least 2 years in length

(2) Minimum starting age of 16

(3) Definite schedule of work processes specified in advance

(4) Organized classroom instruction with a specified number of hour per year to provide technical knowledge related to the trade

(5) Progressive levels of wages as the apprentice proceeds through the program

(6) Proper supervision of on-the-job training

(7) Periodic review and evaluation

(8) Employer-employee cooperation

(9) Recognition for successful completion of the program

Federally, the program is administered by the Bureau of Apprenticeship, a division of the Department of Labor.

There are now apprenticeships in 350 occupations, but the enrollment in apprenticeship programs has not kept pace with the expansion of the needs for skilled workers.

Modern variations of the apprenticeship idea include internships in management, in medicine (in a more advanced form), and in in-service training programs. But as institutions of postsecondary education have increasingly been given the function of preparing persons for occupations, there has been a decrease in the use of apprenticeship for this purpose. In the last two decades, when other forms of postsecondary education have increased dramatically, the number of those in apprenticeship training increased only 25 percent.

The apprenticeship concept should be preserved and improved. It is a particularly intelligent way to prepare persons for work in self-contained crafts or professions. Wherever possible, apprenticeship should be introduced for the new professional and paraprofessional fields that are now emerging. We do urge, however, that the new apprenticeships be well-supported by systematic instruction. Just holding a job may be a learning experience, but it is not necessarily an educational experience. Apprenticeships that are simply a device for controlling access to higher vocational or occupational status are not likely to have educational value.

Specific Objective 11: Apprenticeship, internship, and in-service training will be used more widely than they are today to prepare persons for their life work in many professions, paraprofessions, and occupations.

THE ARMED SERVICES There are seven degree-granting college-level service schools with a combined enrollment in 1970 of 17,036 students.[3] There are also several special-purpose military schools and institutes to which military personnel are sent for short-cycle courses on specific subjects (languages, management, procurement, and contract writing).

Members of the armed forces may voluntarily attend a wide range of classes or enroll in correspondence courses through programs of the United States Armed Forces Institute (USAFI) which, in 1972, offered 200 courses in subjects ranging from basic education to graduate work at the Ph.D. level. In that same year, approximately 175,200 service men and women were enrolled in these courses and another 25,000 members of the armed services were enrolled in courses in educational centers maintained by the University of Maryland and other institutions.

Correspondence instruction is available to military personnel through: (1) the individual services, (2) the United States Armed Forces Institute (USAFI), (3) certain colleges and universities, (4) and some private specialty schools. Courses offered by the services themselves are usually geared to career advancement within the military structure and provide military-oriented training. Courses offered by USAFI and various colleges and universities may be taken for degree credit and, in content, are the same as regular college-level offerings. In 1972, there were over 200,000 military personnel in correspondence courses offered by USAFI and other organizations (Sharon, 1971).

---

[3] U.S. Military Academy, West Point, New York; U.S. Naval Academy, Annapolis, Maryland; U.S. Air Force Academy, Colorado Springs, Colorado; U.S. Coast Guard Academy, New London, Connecticut; U.S. Merchant Marine Academy, Kings Point, New York; Air Force Institute of Technology, Dayton, Ohio; and the U.S. Naval Postgraduate Schools, Monterey, California.

Determination of whether and how much college credit should be given for educational activity pursued by students in military service is a function of the Commission on Accreditation of Service Experiences (CASE), an office of the American Council on Education. CASE does not itself grant credit, but instead makes recommendations to institutions of higher education. In 1970 63 percent of the colleges and universities surveyed by CASE gave credit for service school courses and 72.4 percent gave credit for USAFI courses (CASE *Newsletter,* 1970).

Military personnel may also gain college credit by taking examinations administered by USAFI.

A program developed by the U.S. Department of Defense and the American Association of Community and Junior Colleges places the educational facilities of more than 100 community colleges at the disposal of armed servicemen. These institutions are designated as *Servicemen's Opportunity Colleges* and subscribe to common policies on admissions, contracts with students, and acceptance of credit from other colleges in the program. Completion of required courses through these colleges can lead to an associate in arts degree. A participating serviceman is a "ward" of the institution in which he is initially enrolled, but he is able to acquire credit at other community colleges near bases to which he is transferred.

The American Association of State Colleges and Universities in cooperation with other associations, is working to expand the Serviceman's Opportunity Colleges concept to more generally include four-year institutions. The University of Alaska is already providing evening courses at military installations in the Anchorage area and is supervising similar programs at military stations elsewhere in the state.

In the future, the armed services must be increasingly alert to the post-service career interests of the volunteers. Careful attention must be given, therefore, to the extent to which, through certification requirements, rigid residency requirements, and other policies, the civilian society limits the ability of servicemen to use knowledge and skills learned in the services.

Specific Objective 12: Educational activity provided by the armed forces to officers and enlisted men at postsecondary levels will yield credit that is widely accepted as servicemen are transferred from military base to military base. Some of this instruction will be of a quality that is widely accepted for course credit in civilian educational institutions after the serviceman student is discharged.

Specific Objective 13: The efforts of community colleges and four-year colleges to provide degree-credit instruction for military personnel and civilians living within commuting distance of such installations will be encouraged and increased.

Specific Objective 14: Enlisted men, as well as officers, will have increasing opportunities to participate in postsecondary education at civilian centers of postsecondary learning through education leave programs subsidized by the armed services.

NATIONAL SERVICE Service programs such as the Peace Corps and VISTA not only serve the national interest and those who are directly benefited by their services but also provide valuable learning experiences for their volunteers. They should, therefore, be attractive alternatives or supplements to college attendance.

In an informal survey conducted by our staff, we obtained the following information about a selected group of such services.

The Peace Corps   Founded in 1961, the Peace Corps operates in 60 countries with 7,000 volunteers in 1973. Volunteers must be 18 years old and the term of service is two years. Since the establishment of the program, 50,000 persons have volunteered. Of those in service in 1973, 70 percent had at least a bachelor's degree. There has been a tendency in recent years to recruit more older persons with well-developed skills. Funding for 1973 was $81 million. Some colleges give credit for Peace Corps service and/or scholarships to returning volunteers.

VISTA   Established in 1965, Volunteers in Service to America had 4,000 volunteers in 1973. There are no educational prerequisites for volunteers over 18, but 53 percent of the volunteers in 1973 were college graduates; 23 percent were high school graduates. About 48 percent of the volunteers are over 25 years old. The normal term of service is one year, but volunteers may re-enlist. Funding for 1973 was $24 million.

University Year for Action   Established in 1971 as part of efforts to enlist higher education in the war on poverty, the University

Year for Action had 1,700 volunteers on 44 campuses in 1973. Institutions give academic credits to the student volunteers to recognize their service activities. During the year of service, volunteers are required to maintain full academic standing. The budget for 1973 was $8.5 million.

Job Corps Established in 1965 as a joint program of the U.S. Departments of the Interior and Labor, the Job Corps had 23,600 participants in 71 centers in 1973. The objective is to educate and equip volunteers with employable skills. Youths may stay in the program for 24 months, but the average length of stay is 5.3 months. It is open to persons 16 to 21 years old. Funding for 1973 was $184.9 million.

Youth Conservation Corps Established in 1970 to provide conservation work and environmental work for youths 15 to 18 years old, in 1973 its programs served about 1,200 youths and 300 staff members in 100 camps. Youths participating in the program serve for 4 to 8 weeks. Funding for 1973 was $5 million.

While we are impressed with the success and potential of the better national service programs, we share the conclusion of the Panel on Youth of the President's Science Advisory Committee (1973) that they provide too few opportunities for participation. According to the panel, "All national programs for youth taken together provided less than 20,000 man-years of opportunity per year. For comparison, the total number of youth aged 18 is currently about 4,000,000." We believe that national service programs should be expanded and should be made more attractive, particularly to persons in the younger age groups. We believe the terms of service should be more flexible and that the reward for service should include financial benefits that can be used in obtaining further education. Such benefits are given now for military service and should be more widely available for other types of service as well.

Specific Objective 15: Local, state, and national governments will provide opportunities for persons to render public service through well-organized programs, and those who engage in national service will be able to earn financial benefits toward education in addition to their regular inservice compensation.

LEARNING PAVILIONS In both urban centers and in remote areas where educational facilities are limited, new types of learning resources are needed. Fortunately, the technology is at hand to make their development possible. As envisioned by the Commission and first described in *The Campus and the City* these resources, called *Learning Pavilions,* can "provide a home base for adult learners, technological aids for independent study, basic educational programs and general educational programs" (Carnegie Commission, 1972, p. 50).

In order to bring facilities within 30 minutes of all residents in an urban center, several learning pavilions would be required. Ideally, they would be located within a metropolitan or branch library complex, although they should seek out cooperation from one or more nearby colleges and universities for instructional support and central communications and computing services. They would emphasize independent study and provide access to such media as audio- and videocassettes, computers, microfiche reachers, independent learning laboratories, and print materials to facilitate such learning (see Appendix A for more details and cost estimates). In this configuration they might contribute almost as much to the learning and culture of the American people at the end of the 20th century as the Carnegie libraries did at the beginning of the century.

Although learning pavilions will have postsecondary education functions, they quite properly should be regarded as community resources and should be substantially funded by the cities or counties in which they are located.

Specific Objective 16: Learning Pavilions designed and operated to encourage and facilitate independent adult learning will be developed in urban centers and in areas that are remote from institutions of postsecondary education. Funding responsibility for construction and operation of such facilities will reside with metropolitan or county governments.

LIBRARIES AND MUSEUMS In our report *The Fourth Revolution: Instructional Technology in Higher Education,* we pointed out that the public libraries and museums of the country are resources for information, illustrations, and other materials that can enrich instruction offered by institutions of higher education. They are particularly valuable as resources for materials that can be used with instructional technology —audio- and videocassettes, film, slides, and live television.

These institutions deserve recognition in their own right, however, as agents of instruction. It is likely that they constitute the most heavily utilized independent learning facilities in the country.

In some areas—Colorado, New York City, and Cleveland, Ohio, in particular, have come to our attention—libraries are beginning to assume a more formal role in the education offered to adults. Some of the programs they provide offer guidance and reading programs specifically directed toward helping learners master knowledge required to earn college credit by examination.

Specific Objective 17: Public libraries and museums will increasingly recognize their potentials as sources for guidance and independent study that can be utilized to meet the standards and objectives of postsecondary-level instruction.

EDUCATION IN PRISONS Although education in prisons is not an optional alternative to colleges or universities, the Carnegie Commission concurs with those who have advocated stronger commitments to education in the prison setting. This commitment is characterized by *"(a)* the recognition that education is an essential element in a modern program of correctional treatment; and *(b)* the belief that such education should be the same type and quality that has been found effective in adult education programs in free society" (Roberts, 1971).

The average daily population of offenders in correctional institutions in the United States is about 400,000. Of this number, between 100,000 and 150,000 are "detained" or serve sentences of such a short duration that it would not be feasible to design educational programs for them. Over 90 percent of these persons are confined in county and local jails and in state prisons. Most county and local jails have no educational programs at all and some state prisons also fall in that category. Federal prisons, which have a population of 20,000 inmates, have identified three goals for their educational program: (1) all inmates leaving the federal prison system will be able to read at least at the sixth grade level, (2) all capable inmates will have a high school equivalency certificate upon release, (3) every inmate with the need will have been trained in a marketable skill.

A recent survey of 46 state and federal prison systems revealed that 36 of the systems had some type of college-level instruction in their educational programs. The most common form was by correspondence study. The second most common was live instruction and visiting college staff followed by instruction via television courses regularly broadcast. A few had recently established college furlough programs which involved busing prisoners to nearby colleges during the day and returning them to prison at night.

The New York state prison system has participated for years in the New York State Department of Education College Proficiency Examination, which permits an inmate to earn up to two years' college credit.

While the incidence of college programs in prisons is fairly large, the average size of student bodies is quite small. Nine of the prison systems programs that provided live instruction had total student involvement of less than 30.

In a few system the Department of Vocational Rehabilitation has provided funds for the support of educational programs. In all of the systems that include more than a handful of inmates, the amount of payment by the inmate is negligible.

A large number of the live instruction college-level courses are subsidized either through normal junior college funding arrangements, or through the department of correction, or through vocational rehabilitation departments. In one system, an annual prison rodeo pays for a portion of the instruction costs.

Specific Objective 18: Educational institutions located within accessible range of prisons and having at their disposal well-developed instructional technology will make remote-access instruction and independent learning materials available to prison education programs at minimum costs.

INTER-INSTI-TUTIONAL CONTRACTUAL ARRANGE-MENTS

While there are differences among the educational missions of various institutions and agencies operating in postsecondary education, these differences are not, nor should they be, so discreetly drawn that the mission of one agency or institution does not overlap with the missions of any other agencies or institutions. But in such situations, there does seem to be a natural tendency for each of the institutions to expand its own framework to include more and more of the total range of possible educational missions in postsecondary education. This tendency is reinforced at the present time when many learners are broadening the range of their own educational goals. And, to the extent that all institutions try to supply directly all educational needs, individual institutions lose their capacity for making unique contributions to particular educational needs.

Specific Objective 19: Before taking on a new educational function, institutions will determine the relationship of that function to their educational mission and will ascertain whether there are existing alternative educational resources to meet the particular educationa need to be served. If such alternative resources exist, the possi bility of contractual agreements with other institutions to secur the services, or the possibility of joint enrollment of the learner will be explored before a new program is developed.

7. Conclusion

A distinguishing feature of the new era for postsecondary education in the United States is that there will be more students of all ages. Many of the new learners will be older than those customarily regarded as of college age. But some of them will be younger persons who prefer more flexible forms of education than are now generally available at colleges and universities.

COSTS: TOTAL
Because enrollments will be increased by these new learners, costs for colleges and universities will increase. The Commission's current estimates of enrollments indicate a 1980–81 enrollment (FTE) of 8.8 million and current expenditures of $41.5 billion (in 1970–71 dollars), assuming a 10 percent improvement over trend in cost per FTE student.

In this report, we have made many recommendations that should make colleges and universities more attractive as sources of learning for the "new learners" anticipated in the coming decades. Not the least of these recommendations is that consideration be given to providing every individual in the country with two years education "in the bank" for use at any time of their lives. We believe that if the recommendations in this report—exclusive of the two-years-in-the-bank idea—are adopted, full-time-equivalent enrollments will reach 8.9 million by 1980–81. If the two-years-in-the-bank idea were adopted the enrollment would be much greater than that. The total cost of such enrollments would be $42.0 billion—about $600 million more than we recommended on the basis of the enrollment projection in our 1972 report on *The More Effective Use of Resources*. To these costs must be added any costs for expansion of facilities, introduction of alternative modes of instruction, and greater utilization of instructional technology that might occur in the implementation of our recommendations in this report.

But the full burden of instruction will not be borne by colleges and universities alone. In this report we have described several alternatives to academic institutions as sources of education for a learning society, and we have urged that these be considered seriously by all prospective students. To the extent that public subsidies are extended to students who participate in such institutions — particularly private specialty schools and correspondence schools — public expenditures related to postsecondary education will obviously increase in proportion to the number of students assisted and the amounts of aid provided. We also have recommended the creation of learning pavilions in urban areas to encourage and facilitate independent learning by students of all ages. Creating such facilities initially adequate to the needs of our 50 largest cities would require new expenditures of about $150 million for capital costs, and $50 to $60 million annually for operation.[1]

COSTS:
PER CHANNEL
In determining the relative costs of the various channels to life, work, and service some care is required to identify the vantage point from which the estimate is made. From the vantage point of institutional expenditures alone, the resident college student, who averages two years in college (allowing for dropouts) necessitates an annual expenditure of about $2,500 for his education. Alan Pifer has pointed out that the average cost in a recent year of having a person serve in VISTA or the Peace Corps was about $7,800 and $10,000 respectively (Pifer, 1971, p. 14). In 1970, the "basic pay and allowances" for the average person on active duty in the military services was $5,759 (U.S. Bureau of the Census, 1972, p. 263). If food and lodging were completely included, the amount spent would probably be close to $7,500 a year.

From the point of view of what it costs society (including the individual) to learn rather than earn or produce things, it is useful to assume some average duration of participation and then cost out the value of instructional services plus forgone earnings (or loss of production). On this basis, the following range of typical costs for full-time-equivalent participation in each program have been estimated by our staff:

[1] These figures assume an average of five centers per city. It is unlikely all of them would, or should, be built in the same year.

Program and degree of participation, 1970–71 dollars	Average instructional costs (1)	Estimated forgone earnings (2)	Estimated economic cost	
			Total (1) & (2) (3)	Per week (3) ÷ weeks (4)
1 FTE year (36–40 weeks) of college	$2,400	$3,400	$5,800	$145–161
16 weeks of initial and advanced military training	2,000	2,700	4,700	294
1 year (50 weeks) of registered apprenticeship	400	150	550	11
1 FTE year (36–40 weeks) of public postsecondary nondegree studies (in community colleges and area vocational-technical schools)	1,800	1,900	3,700	92–102
1 FTE year (36–40 weeks) of study in a private specialty school	1,600	1,200	2,800	70–77

In the above estimates, the costs for college are comparatively high because longer periods per day are spent in class and very high forgone earning are involved. The costs of military training are higher because instruction occurs during much of an eight-hour day, separate facilities are used to house "students," and we have assumed that society forgoes the possibility of national defense services that would be produced if those taking instruction were not in training. The costs of apprenticeships are low because it is assumed that the alternative to study as an apprentice would simply be to spend one's time working at about the same rate of pay received as an apprentice; moreover, the time actually spent in classroom instruction is relatively short and frequently occurs in hours of slack production. The costs for private specialty schools are lower than for colleges because most students at these institutions work full- or part-time and therefore have smaller forgone earnings than college students. Moreover, their costs of instruction per hour in the classroom are probably lower. We have not included data on national service programs in these comparisons because the magnitude of these channels is not yet large enough to make comparison meaningful.

PRIORITIES FOR ACTION

The priorities for action as we see them, are:

- At the federal level

Expansion of support for national service programs and provision for educational credit upon completion

Encouragement of experimentation with educational technology

Enlargement of the educational component in the military service

Establishment of a validation system to protect use of federal monies and against fraud

Expansion of student support systems to cover students of all ages attending more types of institutions

Consideration of an extended support system in the direction of an "educational endowment" or "two years of education in the bank" available throughout life.

- At the state level

  Improved and broadened mechanisms for coordination of postsecondary education

  Protection against fraud by profit-making agencies

  Extension of the community college system

- At the city level

  Creation of counseling and guidance services for persons seeking educational opportunities

  Support of learning pavilions

- For higher education

  More options for students to move into and out of formal education

  More acceptance of part-time students and adults—no minimum credit hours, no upper age limits

  More attention to the definition of academic standards, particularly in accreditation and in evaluation of experiential learning

- For employers

  More attention to cumulative records and less to degrees earned except where the specific degree is essential to the specific job. There should be more respect for competence however obtained and less for the particular method by which it is developed.

Fortunately, the learning society is emerging at a time when our colleges and universities and other institutions of postsecondary education are best able to deal with it. The rapid, almost frantic growth of the 1950s and 1960s is over. Many states have created coordinating agencies that can be used for planning and developing the diversity of channels and opportunities that are needed to serve new students in the new age of learning. Teachers are readily available. It is urgent that we proceed with such plans and developments; the present opportunity to act constructively should not be allowed to pass unheeded.

Appendix A: Suggested Facilities and Estimated Costs for Learning Pavilions

The facilities of a typical learning pavilion might include:

A central individual study room with carrels for videocassette players, graphic computer terminals, and electronic calculators. Lounge chairs would be provided for reading and for use of more compact learning devices.

Seminar rooms which can accommodate up to 20 students.

Tutorial rooms which can be used for brief meetings between tutors and up to five students.

Counseling offices for counselors who work with the students in defining learning goals and assisting them in entering the instructional program of their choice.

Administrative offices

Technical support and storage room which provides facilities for maintenance of equipment used at the center and for storage of equipment and materials not currently in use.

Typing rooms to be used by students for typing reports and other documents related to their studies.

Child care center A supervised playroom where married students can leave preschool children while they study. (The supervisor of this room would be paid out of fees collected from parents using the service.)

Parking lot

NOTE: The materials presented in this appendix are adapted from *Flying a Learning Center,* by Thomas J. Karwin, coordinator of instructional services, University of California, Santa Cruz. This document will soon be issued by the Carnegie Commission on Higher Education as a technical report.

The typical center would operate on a twelve-hour day, six-day week, twelve-month year schedule. For such a pavilion designed to accommodate 1,000 half-time students (on a head-count basis), it is estimated that capital costs would be $450,000 plus costs of land acquisition. Operating costs would be $226,070 per year. Not included in the cost estimates are books for the library and the costs of other courseware. Cost estimates also assume that the pavilions will be served by on-line computer facilities and will be able to make use of centralized communications facilities available through their associated campuses.

References

American Council on Education: *Higher Education and the Adult Student,* Washington, D.C., October 25, 1972.

Belitsky, A. Harvey: *Private Vocational Schools and Their Students,* Schenkman Publishing Co., Inc., Cambridge, Mass., 1969.

Benoit, Richard P.: "Alternative Programs for Higher Education: External and Special Degrees," *Intellect,* pp. 422–425, April 1973.

Bergin, Thomas D.: "Continuing Education in the United States: the Challenge and Responsibility," in Stephen D. Kertesz (ed.), *The Task of Universities in a Changing World,* University of Notre Dame Press, London, 1971.

Carnegie Commission on Higher Education: *The Capitol and the Campus: State Responsibility for Postsecondary Education,* McGraw-Hill Book Company, New York, 1970.

Carnegie Commission on Higher Education: *Less Time, More Options: Education Beyond the High School,* McGraw-Hill Book Company, New York, 1971a.

Carnegie Commission on Higher Education: *New Students and New Places: Policies for the Future Growth and Development of American Higher Education,* McGraw-Hill Book Company, New York, 1971b.

Carnegie Commission on Higher Education: *The Campus and the City: Maximizing Assets and Reducing Liabilities,* McGraw-Hill Book Company, New York, 1972a.

Carnegie Commission on Higher Education: *The Fourth Revolution: Instructional Technology in Higher Education,* McGraw-Hill Book Company, New York, 1972b.

Carnegie Commission on Higher Education: *Reform on Campus: Changing Students, Changing Academic Programs,* McGraw-Hill Book Company, New York, 1972c.

Carnegie Commission on Higher Education: *Higher Education: Who Pays, Who Benefits, Who Should Pay?*, McGraw-Hill Book Company, New York, 1973.

Cartter, Allan: "The Need for a New Approach to Financing Recurrent Education," paper delivered at the Princeton Conference on Post-Degree Continuing Education, May 16, 1973.

CASE *Newsletter*, no. 34, December 1970.

Commission on Non-Traditional Study: *Diversity by Design*, Jossey-Bass, Inc., San Francisco, 1973.

Dresch, Stephen: "U.S. Public Policy and the Evolutionary Adaptability of Postsecondary Education," YHERP Report no. 2, comment prepared for the Conference on Recurrent Education, Washington, D.C., March 21, 1973.

Grasso, John T., and John R. Shea: *The Effects of High School Curriculum on Age-Earning Profiles*, Center for Human Resource Research, Ohio State University, Columbus, 1972.

Grasso, John T., and John R. Shea: "The Effects of High School Curriculum on Age-Earning Profiles," *Proceedings of the Social Statistics Section*, American Statistical Association, Montreal, 1973.

Hutchins, Robert M.: *The Learning Society*, Frederick A. Praeger, Inc., New York, 1968.

International Labour Organisation: *Paid Educational Leave*, International Labour Conference, 58th Session, report 6, pt. 1, Geneva, 1972.

Johnstone, John W. C., and Ramon J. Rivera: *Volunteers for Learning: A Study of Educational Pursuits of American Adults*, a NORC Research Study, Aldine Publishing Company, Chicago, 1965.

Karwin, Thomas J.: *Flying a Learning Center*, 1973. (Mimeograph.)

Lorge, Irving: "Capacities of Older Adults" in Wilma Donahue (ed.), *Education for Later Maturity*, Whiteside Insurance and William From and Co., New York, 1955.

Moses, Stanley: "The 'New' Domain of Postsecondary Education," in *Notes on the Future of Education*, vol. II, Educational Policy Research Center, Syracuse, N.Y., Summer 1971.

National Association of Manufacturers: *Industry-Education Coordinator*, Public Policy Report, New York, 1970.

Owens, William A., and Don C. Charles: *Life History Correlates of Age Changes in Mental Abilities*, Purdue University, Lafayette, Ind., 1963.

Panel on Youth of the President's Science Advisory Committee: *Youth: Transition to Adulthood*, Office of Science and Technology, Washington, 1973.

Parnes, Herbert S., et al.: *Career Thresholds,* vol. I, Manpower Research Monograph no. 16, U.S. Government Printing Office, Washington, D.C., 1970.

Penfield, Kathleen Rockhill: *Academic Excellence vs. Public Service: Conflict and Accommodation Within the University as Revealed in the Development of University Extension at the University of California,* doctoral dissertation, University of California, Berkeley, 1972.

Pifer, Alan: "The Responsibility for Reform in Higher Education," *Annual Report for the Fiscal Year Ended Sept. 30, 1971,* Carnegie Corporation of New York, 1971.

Rehn, Gösta: *Prospective View on Patterns of Working Time,* report no. 1B, International Conference on New Patterns for Working Time, Organisation for Economic Co-operation and Development, Paris, 1972.

Roberts, Albert R.: *Source book on Prison Education,* Charles C. Thomas, Publisher, Springfield, Ill., 1971.

Sharon, Amiel T.: *College Credit for Off-Campus Study,* report 8, ERIC Clearinghouse on Higher Education, George Washington University, Washington, D.C., March 1971.

Somers, Gerald, and Myron Roomkin: *Training and Skill Acquisition: A Pilot Case Study,* contract 81-55-71-04, Manpower Administration, U.S. Department of Labor, Manpower and Training Research Unit, affiliated with the Industrial Relations Research Center and the Center for Studies in Vocational and Technical Education, University of Wisconsin, Madison, 1972.

Study on Continuing Education and the Future: *The Learning Society: A Report of the Study on Continuing Education and the Future,* Center of Continuing Education, Notre Dame, 1973.

Tobin, James, and Leonard Ross: "Paying for the High Costs of Education: A National Youth Endowment," *New Republic,* vol. 160, pp. 18–21, May 3, 1969.

Torpey, William G.: "Company Investment in Continuing Education for Scientists and Engineers," *Educational Record,* Fall 1964.

Tyler, Ralph W.: "Cooperative Education—Values and Objectives," *AGB Reports,* vol. 15, no. 3, Nov.–Dec., 1972.

U.S. Bureau of the Census: "Projection of the Population of the United States by Age and Sex: 1970 to 2020," *Current Population Reports,* ser. P-25, no. 470, 1971.

U.S. Bureau of Labor Statistics: "Employment of High School Graduates and Dropouts," *Special Labor Force Reports,* nos. 121, 131, and 145, reprinted in *Monthly Labor Review,* August 1970; May 1971; and May 1972.

U.S. Office of Education: *Participation in Adult Education,* Circular 539. 1959.

U.S. Office of Education, National Center for Educational Statistics: *Participation in Adult Education,* 1969, initial reports, OE 72-1, 1971.

Wilson, James W.: "Cooperative Education — Historical Perspectives," *AGB Reports,* vol. 15, no. 3, Nov.–Dec., 1972.

Carnegie Commission on Higher Education

Sponsored Research Studies

THE FUTURE OF HIGHER EDUCATION:
SOME SPECULATIONS AND SUGGESTIONS
Alexander M. Mood

CONTENT AND CONTEXT:
ESSAYS ON COLLEGE EDUCATION
Carl Kaysen (ed.)

THE RISE OF THE ARTS ON THE AMERICAN
CAMPUS
Jack Morrison

THE UNIVERSITY AND THE CITY:
EIGHT CASES OF INVOLVEMENT
*George Nash, Dan Waldorf, and Robert E.
Price*

THE BEGINNING OF THE FUTURE:
A HISTORICAL APPROACH TO GRADUATE
EDUCATION IN THE ARTS AND SCIENCES
Richard J. Storr

ACADEMIC TRANSFORMATION:
SEVENTEEN INSTITUTIONS UNDER PRESSURE
David Riesman and Verne A. Stadtman (eds.)

THE UNIVERSITY AS AN ORGANIZATION
James A. Perkins (ed.)

NEW DIRECTIONS IN LEGAL EDUCATION
*Herbert L. Packer and Thomas Ehrlich
abridged and unabridged editions*

WHERE COLLEGES ARE AND WHO ATTENDS:
EFFECTS OF ACCESSIBILITY ON COLLEGE
ATTENDANCE
*C. Arnold Anderson, Mary Jean Bowman, and
Vincent Tinto*

THE EMERGING TECHNOLOGY:
INSTRUCTIONAL USE OF THE COMPUTER IN
HIGHER EDUCATION
Roger Levien

A STATISTICAL PORTRAIT OF HIGHER
EDUCATION
Seymour E. Harris

THE HOME OF SCIENCE:
THE ROLE OF THE UNIVERSITY
Dael Wolfle

EDUCATION AND EVANGELISM:
A PROFILE OF PROTESTANT COLLEGES
C. Robert Pace

PROFESSIONAL EDUCATION:
SOME NEW DIRECTIONS
Edgar H. Schein

THE NONPROFIT RESEARCH INSTITUTE:
ITS ORIGIN, OPERATION, PROBLEMS, AND
PROSPECTS
Harold Orlans

THE INVISIBLE COLLEGES:
A PROFILE OF SMALL, PRIVATE COLLEGES
WITH LIMITED RESOURCES
Alexander W. Astin and Calvin B. T. Lee

A DEGREE AND WHAT ELSE?:
CORRELATES AND CONSEQUENCES OF A
COLLEGE EDUCATION
*Stephen B. Withey, Jo Anne Coble, Gerald
Gurin, John P. Robinson, Burkhard Strumpel,
Elizabeth Keogh Taylor, and Arthur C. Wolfe*

THE MULTICAMPUS UNIVERSITY:
A STUDY OF ACADEMIC GOVERNANCE
Eugene C. Lee and Frank M. Bowen

INSTITUTIONS IN TRANSITION:
A PROFILE OF CHANGE IN HIGHER
EDUCATION
(INCORPORATING THE 1970 STATISTICAL
REPORT)
Harold L. Hodgkinson

EFFICIENCY IN LIBERAL EDUCATION:
A STUDY OF COMPARATIVE INSTRUCTIONAL
COSTS FOR DIFFERENT WAYS OF ORGANIZ-
ING TEACHING-LEARNING IN A LIBERAL ARTS
COLLEGE
Howard R. Bowen and Gordon K. Douglass

CREDIT FOR COLLEGE:
PUBLIC POLICY FOR STUDENT LOANS
Robert W. Hartman

MODELS AND MAVERICKS:
A PROFILE OF PRIVATE LIBERAL ARTS
COLLEGES
Morris T. Keeton

BETWEEN TWO WORLDS:
A PROFILE OF NEGRO HIGHER EDUCATION
Frank Bowles and Frank A. DeCosta

BREAKING THE ACCESS BARRIERS:
A PROFILE OF TWO-YEAR COLLEGES
Leland L. Medsker and Dale Tillery

ANY PERSON, ANY STUDY:
AN ESSAY ON HIGHER EDUCATION IN THE
UNITED STATES
Eric Ashby

THE NEW DEPRESSION IN HIGHER
EDUCATION:
A STUDY OF FINANCIAL CONDITIONS AT 41
COLLEGES AND UNIVERSITIES
Earl F. Cheit

FINANCING MEDICAL EDUCATION:
AN ANALYSIS OF ALTERNATIVE POLICIES
AND MECHANISMS
Rashi Fein and Gerald I. Weber

HIGHER EDUCATION IN NINE COUNTRIES:
A COMPARATIVE STUDY OF COLLEGES AND
UNIVERSITIES ABROAD
*Barbara B. Burn, Philip G. Altbach, Clark Kerr,
and James A. Perkins*

BRIDGES TO UNDERSTANDING:
INTERNATIONAL PROGRAMS OF AMERICAN
COLLEGES AND UNIVERSITIES
Irwin T. Sanders and Jennifer C. Ward

GRADUATE AND PROFESSIONAL EDUCATION,
1980:
A SURVEY OF INSTITUTIONAL PLANS
Lewis B. Mayhew

THE AMERICAN COLLEGE AND AMERICAN
CULTURE:
SOCIALIZATION AS A FUNCTION OF HIGHER
EDUCATION
Oscar Handlin and Mary F. Handlin

RECENT ALUMNI AND HIGHER EDUCATION:
A SURVEY OF COLLEGE GRADUATES
Joe L. Spaeth and Andrew M. Greeley

CHANGE IN EDUCATIONAL POLICY:
SELF-STUDIES IN SELECTED COLLEGES AND
UNIVERSITIES
Dwight R. Ladd

STATE OFFICIALS AND HIGHER EDUCATION:
A SURVEY OF THE OPINIONS AND
EXPECTATIONS OF POLICY MAKERS IN NINE
STATES
Heinz Eulau and Harold Quinley

ACADEMIC DEGREE STRUCTURES:
INNOVATIVE APPROACHES
PRINCIPLES OF REFORM IN DEGREE
STRUCTURES IN THE UNITED STATES
Stephen H. Spurr

COLLEGES OF THE FORGOTTEN AMERICANS:
A PROFILE OF STATE COLLEGES AND
REGIONAL UNIVERSITIES
E. Alden Dunham

FROM BACKWATER TO MAINSTREAM:
A PROFILE OF CATHOLIC HIGHER
EDUCATION
Andrew M. Greeley

THE ECONOMICS OF THE MAJOR PRIVATE
UNIVERSITIES
William G. Bowen
*(Out of print, but available from University
Microfilms.)*

THE FINANCE OF HIGHER EDUCATION
Howard R. Bowen
*(Out of print, but available from University
Microfilms.)*

ALTERNATIVE METHODS OF FEDERAL
FUNDING FOR HIGHER EDUCATION
Ron Wolk
(Out of print, but available from University
Microfilms.)

INVENTORY OF CURRENT RESEARCH ON
HIGHER EDUCATION 1968
Dale M. Heckman and Warren Bryan Martin
(Out of print, but available from University
Microfilms.)

The following technical reports are available from the Carnegie Commission on Higher Education, 2150
Shattuck Avenue, Berkeley, California 94704.

RESOURCE USE IN HIGHER EDUCATION:
TRENDS IN OUTPUT AND INPUTS, 1930–1967
June O'Neill

TRENDS AND PROJECTIONS OF PHYSICIANS
IN THE UNITED STATES 1967–2002
Mark S. Blumberg

MAY 1970:
THE CAMPUS AFTERMATH OF CAMBODIA
AND KENT STATE
Richard E. Peterson and John A. Bilorusky

MENTAL ABILITY AND HIGHER EDUCATIONAL
ATTAINMENT IN THE 20TH CENTURY
Paul Taubman and Terence Wales

AMERICAN COLLEGE AND UNIVERSITY
ENROLLMENT TRENDS IN 1971
Richard E. Peterson

PAPERS ON EFFICIENCY IN THE
MANAGEMENT OF HIGHER EDUCATION
Alexander M. Mood, Colin Bell,
Lawrence Bogard, Helen Brownlee,
and Joseph McCloskey

AN INVENTORY OF ACADEMIC INNOVATION
AND REFORM
Ann Heiss

ESTIMATING THE RETURNS TO EDUCATION:
A DISAGGREGATED APPROACH
Richard S. Eckaus

SOURCES OF FUNDS TO COLLEGES AND
UNIVERSITIES
June O'Neill

NEW DEPRESSION IN HIGHER
EDUCATION—TWO YEARS LATER
Earl F. Cheit

PROFESSORS, UNIONS, AND AMERICAN
HIGHER EDUCATION
Everett Carll Ladd, Jr. and Seymour Martin
Lipset

The following reprints are available from the Carnegie Commission on Higher Education, 2150 Shattuck
Avenue, Berkeley, California 94704.

ACCELERATED PROGRAMS OF MEDICAL EDUCATION, by Mark S. Blumberg, reprinted from
JOURNAL OF MEDICAL EDUCATION, vol. 46, no. 8, August 1971.*

SCIENTIFIC MANPOWER FOR 1970–1985, by Allan M. Cartter, reprinted from SCIENCE, vol.
172, no. 3979, pp. 132–140, April 9, 1971.

A NEW METHOD OF MEASURING STATES' HIGHER EDUCATION BURDEN, by Neil Timm, reprinted
from THE JOURNAL OF HIGHER EDUCATION, vol. 42, no. 1, pp. 27–33, January 1971.*

REGENT WATCHING, by Earl F. Cheit, reprinted from AGB REPORTS, vol. 13, no. 6, pp. 4–13,
March 1971.

COLLEGE GENERATIONS—FROM THE 1930s TO THE 1960s by Seymour M. Lipset and Everett
C. Ladd, Jr., reprinted from THE PUBLIC INTEREST, no. 25, Summer 1971.

AMERICAN SOCIAL SCIENTISTS AND THE GROWTH OF CAMPUS POLITICAL ACTIVISM IN THE
1960s, by Everett C. Ladd, Jr., and Seymour M. Lipset, reprinted from SOCIAL SCIENCES
INFORMATION, vol. 10, no. 2, April 1971.

THE POLITICS OF AMERICAN POLITICAL SCIENTISTS, *by Everett C. Ladd, Jr., and Seymour M. Lipset, reprinted from* PS, *vol. 4, no. 2, Spring 1971.**

THE DIVIDED PROFESSORIATE, *by Seymour M. Lipset and Everett C. Ladd, Jr., reprinted from* CHANGE, *vol. 3, no. 3, pp. 54–60, May 1971.**

JEWISH ACADEMICS IN THE UNITED STATES: THEIR ACHIEVEMENTS, CULTURE AND POLITICS, *by Seymour M. Lipset and Everett C. Ladd, Jr., reprinted from* AMERICAN JEWISH YEAR BOOK, *1971.*

THE UNHOLY ALLIANCE AGAINST THE CAMPUS, *by Kenneth Keniston and Michael Lerner, reprinted from* NEW YORK TIMES MAGAZINE, *November 8, 1970 .*

PRECARIOUS PROFESSORS: NEW PATTERNS OF REPRESENTATION, *by Joseph W. Garbarino, reprinted from* INDUSTRIAL RELATIONS, *vol. 10, no. 1, February 1971.**

. . . AND WHAT PROFESSORS THINK: ABOUT STUDENT PROTEST AND MANNERS, MORALS, POLITICS, AND CHAOS ON THE CAMPUS, *by Seymour Martin Lipset and Everett C. Ladd, Jr., reprinted from* PSYCHOLOGY TODAY, *November 1970.**

DEMAND AND SUPPLY IN U.S. HIGHER EDUCATION: A PROGRESS REPORT, *by Roy Radner and Leonard S. Miller, reprinted from* AMERICAN ECONOMIC REVIEW, *May 1970.**

RESOURCES FOR HIGHER EDUCATION: AN ECONOMIST'S VIEW, *by Theodore W. Schultz, reprinted from* JOURNAL OF POLITICAL ECONOMY, *vol. 76, no. 3, University of Chicago, May/June 1968.**

INDUSTRIAL RELATIONS AND UNIVERSITY RELATIONS, *by Clark Kerr, reprinted from* PROCEEDINGS OF THE 21ST ANNUAL WINTER MEETING OF THE INDUSTRIAL RELATIONS RESEARCH ASSOCIATION, *pp. 15–25.**

NEW CHALLENGES TO THE COLLEGE AND UNIVERSITY, *by Clark Kerr, reprinted from Kermit Gordon (ed.),* AGENDA FOR THE NATION, *The Brookings Institution, Washington, D.C., 1968.**

PRESIDENTIAL DISCONTENT, *by Clark Kerr, reprinted from David C. Nichols (ed.),* PERSPECTIVES ON CAMPUS TENSIONS: PAPERS PREPARED FOR THE SPECIAL COMMITTEE ON CAMPUS TENSIONS, *American Council on Education, Washington, D.C., September 1970.**

STUDENT PROTEST—AN INSTITUTIONAL AND NATIONAL PROFILE, *by Harold Hodgkinson, reprinted from* THE RECORD, *vol. 71, no. 4, May 1970.**

WHAT'S BUGGING THE STUDENTS?, *by Kenneth Keniston, reprinted from* EDUCATIONAL RECORD, *American Council on Education, Washington, D.C., Spring 1970.**

THE POLITICS OF ACADEMIA, *by Seymour Martin Lipset, reprinted from David C. Nichols (ed.),* PERSPECTIVES ON CAMPUS TENSIONS: PAPERS PREPARED FOR THE SPECIAL COMMITTEE ON CAMPUS TENSIONS, *American Council on Education, Washington, D.C., September 1970.**

INTERNATIONAL PROGRAMS OF U.S. COLLEGES AND UNIVERSITIES: PRIORITIES FOR THE SEVEN-TIES, *by James A. Perkins, reprinted by permission of the International Council for Educational Development, Occasional Paper no. 1, July 1971.*

FACULTY UNIONISM: FROM THEORY TO PRACTICE, *by Joseph W. Garbarino, reprinted from* INDUSTRIAL RELATIONS, *vol. 11, no. 1, pp. 1–17, February 1972.*

MORE FOR LESS: HIGHER EDUCATION'S NEW PRIORITY, *by Virginia B. Smith, reprinted from* UNIVERSAL HIGHER EDUCATION: COSTS AND BENEFITS, *American Council on Education, Washington, D.C., 1971.*

ACADEMIA AND POLITICS IN AMERICA, *by Seymour M. Lipset, reprinted from Thomas J. Nossiter (ed.),* IMAGINATION AND PRECISION IN THE SOCIAL SCIENCES, *pp. 211–289, Faber and Faber, London, 1972.*

POLITICS OF ACADEMIC NATURAL SCIENTISTS AND ENGINEERS, *by Everett C. Ladd, Jr., and Seymour M. Lipset, reprinted from* SCIENCE, *vol. 176, no. 4039, pp. 1091–1100, June 9, 1972.*

THE INTELLECTUAL AS CRITIC AND REBEL: WITH SPECIAL REFERENCE TO THE UNITED STATES AND THE SOVIET UNION, *by Seymour M. Lipset and Richard B. Dobson, reprinted from* DAEDALUS, *vol. 101, no. 3, pp. 137–198, Summer 1972.*

COMING OF MIDDLE AGE IN HIGHER EDUCATION, *by Earl F. Cheit, address delivered to American Association of State Colleges and Universities and National Association of State Universities and Land-Grant Colleges, Washington, D.C., Nov. 13, 1972.*

THE NATURE AND ORIGINS OF THE CARNEGIE COMMISSION ON HIGHER EDUCATION, by Alan Pifer, *reprinted by permission of The Carnegie Commission for the Advancement of Teaching, speech delivered to the Pennsylvania Association of Colleges and Universities, Oct. 16, 1972.*

THE DISTRIBUTION OF ACADEMIC TENURE IN AMERICAN HIGHER EDUCATION, *by Martin Trow, reprinted from* THE TENURE DEBATE, *Bardwell Smith (ed.), Jossey-Bass, San Francisco, 1972.*

THE POLITICS OF AMERICAN SOCIOLOGISTS, *by Seymour M. Lipset, and Everett C. Ladd, Jr., reprinted from* THE AMERICAN JOURNAL OF SOCIOLOGY, *vol. 78, no. 1, July 1972.*

The Commission's stock of this reprint has been exhausted.